WestBow Press books may be ordered through booksellers or by contacting:

WestBow Press
A Division of Thomas Nelson & Zondervan
1663 Liberty Drive
Bloomington, IN 47403
www.westbowpress.com
844-714-3454

Interior Image Credit: Michael Vail

Cover Art Credit by: Karen Myers Frank

ISBN: 978-1-6642-2586-2 (sc)
ISBN: 978-1-6642-2588-6 (hc)
ISBN: 978-1-6642-2587-9 (e)

Library of Congress Control Number: 2021904475

Print information available on the last page.

WestBow Press rev. date: 7/29/2021

The Thing of It Is

Menus and Musings From the
Life of a Centenarian Saint

LISA MCGOVERN

WESTBOW
PRESS®
A DIVISION OF THOMAS NELSON
& ZONDERVAN

Contents

"There is no good trying to be more spiritual than God. God never meant man to be a purely spiritual creature. That is why He uses material things like bread and wine to put the new life into us. We may think this rather crude and unspiritual. God does not: He invented eating. He likes matter. He invented it."
~C.S. Lewis
Mere Christianity

Introduction

This is a book about nourishment: feeding souls and feeding bodies. The difference is often negligible. It arose from the inspiring life of an extraordinarily ordinary woman, Mabel Sawhill, who made it her life's purpose to minister to people by feeding them. Mabel was not a chef and had no formal culinary training. She was an Iowa farm-girl who came to the Maryland suburbs of Washington, D.C. during WWII to serve her country and her God by working for the Navy. Throughout her 103 years, Mabel's life became the stuff of local legend.

Most folks remember Mabel traipsing around a kitchen, getting the food ready for a gathering: a wedding, a church meeting, a ladies' club brunch. Always dressed to the nines, she clicked and clacked in her kitten heels to survey the banquet line. If she didn't know everybody in the line, she would do her best to get to know them before the event was over. We all marveled at the energy and efficiency with which she masterminded these events, at times for hundreds. Even in her nineties, Mabel's energy matched that of someone half her age.

We—myself, my husband, others who knew and loved Mabel— wanted to know how to do what she did, because after all, even Mabel Sawhill would not live forever. So I encouraged her to jot down some of her closely guarded recipes; she reluctantly produced a few, and thus began our collaboration on this project. When we began, she still wore her high-heeled pink leopard print shoes with a matching bag to church weekly, a practice she continued well into her nineties.

If she was reluctant to share recipes, she was not reluctant to share her stories: stories of her life, her faith, her unending gratitude for all that God had done for her in her life. This started out as a book to teach folks how to cook the way Mabel did, but became a book about finding joy as we serve others, even when we do not feel particularly equipped to do so. Mabel's joy was rooted in serving others in the most basic, most necessary way: by feeding them. And since most folks love to eat, Mabel's recipes created opportunities for people to gather, where—sometimes without even knowing it—they were ministered to, encouraged, and inspired to live joyfully and do all things to the glory of God. Her stories are wrapped in recipes that are served with encouragement to live joyfully and do everything to the glory of God.

Something unexpected happens when we live alongside the venerable elder saints among us. As I was drawn into Mabel's kitchen, I witnessed the beauty of strong, wrinkled, bent hands, floured and sticky as they served. I experienced the lightened burden of shared work transformed into joy. Days filled with sticky buns and strawberry spinach salad became profound lessons in gratitude for the grace of God in our own lives. Although my husband Frank and I were relative latecomers into Mabel's life—we only met her when she was in her late 80s—her impact on our lives will no doubt stretch into eternity.

As her floured hands rolled out the dough for sticky buns, Mabel shared with us the stories familiar to all who knew her: her escapades growing up on the farm in Iowa, her wartime transition to D.C. life, her capers among all kinds of folks as the catering chapter of her life took root. Every story Mabel told had a singular purpose: she wanted folks to know the great things God had done for her and bring glory to Him. Although she was rarely averse to admiration of her chicken salad or her latest Nordstrom bag, the chief desire of her heart was always to sing God's praises.

Although Mabel loved to put on a nice event, her vision was larger than the event itself. She was always on the lookout for kitchen helpers who could also shred chicken and lift pans of sticky buns while being encouraged, entertained, and stealthily discipled with stories of her walk with Jesus. Frank and I, newcomers to Wallace Presbyterian Church when we met Mabel in 2001, must have looked like we needed some of that encouragement. When she saw our family of five filing into a pew near the front every week, looking a little ragged, she figured we could use a little of her kitchen therapy.

We were unlikely recruits; neither of us had any experience catering, nor did we have much of an inclination to do much more than we absolutely had to in our own kitchen, let alone anyone else's. We were in that season of life where the margins were narrow as we tried to keep up with the seemingly endless demands of work and family: we were in survival mode. The last thing I felt I had time or energy to do was to think about serving beautiful, tasty food to other people.

Mabel sensed our exhaustion, and, as she did with so many folks, began to gently and persistently point us closer toward the only One who could truly give us any rest. She sought us out to be her kitchen helpers—who could possibly say no to the feisty 80-year-old?—and we began to cherish these times of working alongside her in church kitchens, in camp kitchens, in women's clubs, and in people's homes. By inviting us to minister with her, she ministered to us, in ways that we continue to discover even though she is no longer with us.

As we worked alongside Mabel, we began to marvel at her ceaseless energy and zealous desire to serve God by using her gifts and resources to serve others. These times with Mabel, much more than serving dinners or learning to prepare food for a crowd, became occasions of sweet fellowship and discipleship.

Gradually, some sparks of Mabel's spirit of hospitality began to burn away the hard edges of my attitude about serving folks about the table. Whether feeding my family each evening, preparing holiday meals, or dishing up casseroles at the church pot-luck, I had never considered hospitality my gift. But I caught a bit of Mabel's joy (and hopefully a few of her skills) and began to cherish the memories of chopping vegetables, rolling dough, and shredding chicken with laughter and love. Although she taught me a lot about how somebody with little talent or inclination could prepare simple, tasty meals for many people, most of Mabel's legacy to me reaches far beyond the kitchen: understanding the significance of the work we do every day, no matter what it is; learning to serve God by serving the people he brings around us; remembering the goodness and holiness of food and our bodies; and grasping the joy and delight we can and should enjoy every day, now, in this broken, beautiful, absolutely redeemable world. Now I try to bring a bit of Mabel into whatever culinary escapades are set before me to do. Sometimes that means the daily grind of mealtimes, sometimes it means a precious gathering of my grown children and their little ones, sometimes it means sweating in a camp kitchen at the youth group retreat to minister to teenagers. The actual food we eat, I have learned, is of less consequence than I thought it would be, and the fact of having shared it around a table is of far more consequence than I had thought it would be.

My hope is that these stories, observations, recipes, and menus from Mabel will bring you encouragement to battle through the everyday weariness that plagues us all sometimes and will exhort you to love folks by feeding them in your homes, offices, churches, homeless shelters, or anyplace else you're needed. And I pray that as you carry out this important work, the Lord will bless you richly with sweet fellowship of old friends, the delight of new friends, and the comfort and joy of family gathered around a table.

As Mabel has taught so many of us, it's not really the food the matters. It's the breaking bread together that feeds us, body and soul.

We need to care for each other as we each navigate the journey set before us. What more basic, necessary, nurturing gesture can there be than to share a meal? It is what we do instinctively at key moments in life. When somebody dies, we bring food to the family; this is how we mourn together. When a baby is born, we bring food for the new mom; this is how we give her rest. When a neighbor is recovering from surgery, we take a meal to him; this is how we offer hope and healing. When a friend has a broken heart, we share a meal; this is how we enter into her pain and share the burden.

When we feed people, we mimic the provision with which God has sustained his people, and we get a foretaste of what He promises to do at the end of all things. He provided manna for the Israelites in the desert; He provided flour and oil that did not run out for the destitute widow at Zarephath. A wedding feast was the scene of Jesus' first public miracle, and we know that all will be set right again someday at the glorious marriage feast of the Lamb. When we feast, we enter the realm of the divine. Preparing, sharing, and providing food are life-giving endeavors whenever and wherever they happen. We experience the sacredness of food and feasting when we gather around the communion table on Sundays to partake of the bread and wine that symbolize Christ's gift of life to us every time we gather around our dining tables and banquet tables to break bread together.

Food is comfort; food is celebration; food is commemoration. But it is also the stuff of our everyday lives. The need for our daily bread causes families to gather around the table at the end of the day, gives colleagues a chance to break from work and talk to each other over a sandwich, and provides friends an occasion to break from the cares of life and re-connect. And although we no doubt enjoy the grand meals and the special occasions, it is mostly in the daily provision that we experience the most profound gratitude. Most of us have no expectations for a culinary masterpiece for our daily meals but are instead mostly happy with whatever satisfies our hunger. The gourmet meal, the sumptuous buffet, the chicken casserole in an aluminum pan delivered to a sick friend, the Thursday night leftovers—there is beauty in all of it. When we feed others, we're fed ourselves: we're all revived and caught up in the deliciousness of living. I hope as you read these stories and reflections that you will come to realize, as I have, that food is not merely fuel to keep our physical bodies going, but is a gift from God that can nurture people's souls and point them toward the Great Gift-Giver.

"The thing of it is," Mabel would say, "everyone needs to eat, so you might as well enjoy it."

Notes on Recipes/ Menus/ Instructions

In addition to Mabel's stories and my reflections on these pages, you will find recipes and menus. The recipes were especially hard to come by: not only was Mabel reluctant to give up the secrets that made her a storied centenarian catering dynamo, she also rarely followed recipes. She had done this work for so long that her plans transcended any kind of written formula.

Because Mabel didn't often follow recipes, her food prep could not be considered precise. But, with few exceptions, what she cooked tasted good, and she always prepared enough to feed everybody. If you've ever been in charge of feeding a crowd, especially a crowd that is not particularly in tune to the purpose of a good old-fashioned RSVP, you know that it is not an insignificant feat to ensure that nobody goes away hungry. After decades of preparing food for banquets, weddings, meetings, and showers, Mabel's intuition became so fine-tuned that she could practically prepare the event's menu on auto-pilot.

When we began the project of this book together, Mabel was in her late 90s and eager to make sure her legacy of hospitality would live on after she was no longer with us. So she dug out an old folder of recipes, stained and yellowed, and handed them over to me. They have been modified over the years, mostly simplified. The recipes, menus, and instructions in this book come from both the recipes in that folder and my observations from many years working alongside her. Although she was a licensed professional caterer, she saw her cooking as ministry rather than business. She was a servant of God, willing and able to do the thing set before her to do. Her food was definitely not haute cuisine; like the Depression-era Iowa farm from which she came, it was simple, uncomplicated, and satisfying.

Throughout the book you will find both individual recipes and menus. The recipes are many of what folks told Mabel were their favorites; the menus are taken from occasions or events when I worked with her or was a guest. Even after decades of feeding crowds of people, Mabel was constantly figuring, anticipating, and re-figuring to make sure that everybody was satisfied. It became easier as time went on, she said, because the recipes became second nature to her and she began to recognize which kind of crowd would eat the most of which kind of dish. Her menus are a guide for those of us who are faced with hospitality opportunities but might not feel we have particularly well-developed hospitality gifts. Perhaps these simple, tried and true menus will provide the courage to open our homes or help to orchestrate an event.

Also, please bear in mind that, although these recipes are crowd-tested and approved, they have not undergone the rigorous scrutiny of a professional test kitchen. We have, however, served these recipes as written to many smiling diners on many occasions and have great confidence that you can do the same.

Enjoy!

Prologue

Mabel Lenore Sawhill
October 30, 1913 – April 21, 2017

Mabel Lenore Sawhill was a 4'10" giant of a woman. Her humor, generosity, and spunk served her well through a life that spanned a Great Depression, two world wars, the Civil Rights movement, man's landing on the moon, the digital revolution, and the dawning of the 21st century. Change though the times might, Mabel remained steadfastly guided by her love and commitment to her Lord and to serving her community in whatever ways he provided.

Born October 30, 1913, on her family's farm in Winterset, Iowa, during the administration of Woodrow Wilson—the first of 18 presidents she would see sworn into office—Mabel arrived prematurely and was not expected to survive. But, as she said, "the Great Physician had other plans." Mabel spent her youth on the farm with her two sisters and two brothers, energetically "trying to get lost so that nobody would notice I wasn't doing my chores." Her sense of adventure followed her to Tarkio College in Missouri in 1931, where she majored in sneaking out the fire escape and orchestrating midnight pranks. The Depression nearly jeopardized her chances to finish college, but her father finagled finances so that Mabel could complete her degree. Mabel reminisced gratefully and often for the sacrifices made by her parents on the behalf of their family.

For a 1935 female college graduate, career choices were limited, so upon graduation Mabel returned to DesMoines, Iowa, where she found a position teaching high-schoolers barely younger than herself. She formed life-long relationships during her seven-year tenure at Woodside High

School, enjoying a final reunion with many of them in 2008. Knowing that it was likely their final reunion, Mabel reassured them that they "would meet again, around that Great Throne."

The call to come to the aid of her country during WWII ended her teaching career and brought Mabel to Washington, D.C. in 1942. Although the call to overseas adventure tugged at her heart, she thought she could best serve in our nation's capital. She found a job working for the Department of the Navy, Bureau of Medicine and Surgery, and worked there until her retirement in 1983. During this time, she became a member of Wallace Memorial Presbyterian Church, which became her church home for the rest of her life. She served actively at other area churches as well, meeting needs wherever they arose: first serving church dinners, then catering wedding receptions, and eventually starting her own catering business upon retiring from the Department of the Navy. Many families can claim that Mabel's chicken salad graced several generations of family events: weddings, baby showers, graduations, 50th anniversaries, children's weddings, and funerals. She served midshipmen after the Army-Navy game, school bands at their Spring banquets, women at club meetings, and church members at presbytery meetings. And for more than 50 years, Mabel was the mastermind behind the meals served to teenagers on retreat at Camp Hemlock in the mountains of West Virginia over the Labor Day weekend. Camp menus became so legendary that kids would come just to say they had tasted Mabel's ribs, baked Alaska, and, of course, sticky buns for Sunday morning brunch.

Mabel served others unceasingly and with a flourish: her iconic pink leopard print attire and her colorful shoe wardrobe expressed a fashion sense that transcended an entire century. She was as much invested in the lives of the four-year-old as the fourteen-year-old as the forty-year-old, and beyond. Her kindness and love touched everyone she interacted with. Mabel's acts of kindness, her zest for life, and mostly her immense gratitude to God, will be her perpetual legacy.

Part One
Beginnings

"Is this Heaven?"
"No, it's Iowa."
~Field of Dreams

Mabel Remembers: Life On the Farm

Mabel lived a storied life, but not because of extraordinary talent or spectacular events. She didn't spearhead social or political change on a national level, she wasn't on the forefront of any scientific discoveries, and she wasn't a national celebrity. Her life became the stuff of local legend around the Washington, D.C. area, where she lived, simply because she lived well, she lived long, and she loved God fiercely.

Mabel was proud of her heritage. Although she left her native Iowa and her beloved farm during WWII and never returned to live there fulltime, she always considered herself a simple country girl. Her life, framed by those early days, was rooted in the reality that God is good, hard work is expected, and life is joyful. She was born into an inheritance of a rich legacy of faith and family that laid the foundation for over a century of faithful good work.

It was this legacy that Mabel wanted to be the heart of this book. Along with the folder of recipes, she gave me a second folder full of an assortment of handwritten pages. Here were the highlights of nearly ten decades of life, some written on pages of a yellow legal pad, some on the pages of a pink note pad with flowers vining across the top of the page. The pages tell tales of mischief, disappointment, gratitude, and joyful service.

"I'm no writer," she admitted. "Make the stories sound good."

I pray that what follows not only sounds good, but honors you, Mabel, and mostly that it points readers to the God you love so much.

• ● •

I was born on the family farm in Winterset, Iowa on October 13, 1913, a month earlier than expected, and I was a tiny little thing right from the start. But I like to think that I was also a feisty little thing from that very first day. I was born at home, as was the custom as that time, and weighed a mere four pounds. The survival odds for such a small baby were grim in those early days of the 1900s, but I hung on, cared for tenderly by mother and grandmother, who kept vigil over me day and night.

The situation turned dire, however, at three weeks. As I gasped and wheezed into the night, the family had no choice but to call for the family doctor. He hurried over and delivered the dreaded diagnosis: whooping cough.

"I'm afraid she's not going to make it," Dr. Thompson told my beleaguered family.

• ● •

Mabel loved to tell this story; it was particularly well-suited to her flair for the dramatic. After our church service on Sundays, small crowds gathered to check in, to introduce a new friend, sometimes just to listen. Savoring her place in the spotlight as folk lingered in the sanctuary chairs and in the aisle, she caught up on the news of the week. Often, in our growing congregation, there was news of a birth.

"Fran and Joe's daughter was born on Thursday," came the report, "but she is a bit small. Barely five pounds."

"Oh, that's nothing!" Mabel's bright pink manicured hands flew up into the air. "Let me tell you a story." And we all walked with her, back to 1913 Iowa, and her first fight against the odds.

"My mother and grandmother were like angels, caring for me and trusting that God was in control. Still, they prepared themselves for the worst. But the Great Physician had other plans for me!" she exclaimed. "It's amazing what God can do through us and the people who love us when we rely on Him." She glanced quickly over to see if the young folks were still listening; she especially loved them.

She wanted them to be strong, too, strong of heart, mind, body and soul. She often reasoned that if they knew that this tiny little old lady had been strong for about 100 years, they could be strong, too. "It all comes from God," she continued. Throughout all her days, Mabel readily acknowledged that her life had never been solely in her own hands.

• ● •

Even in those first days as I struggled for my life, my mother and grandmother trusted in the Lord on my behalf and continued to care for me night and day until I finally recovered, proving that good old Iowa stubbornness, deeply rooted family love, and an abiding faith in the Lord was a winning combination.

As a young child, my days were spent at home with my grandmother while my three older siblings, Harold, Iola, and Eleanor, went off to school. Wilbur, the youngest, would come along later. How I loved to crawl into Grandma's lap and read stories together, sitting near a window where we could watch the road to see my siblings coming toward home at the end of the school day, swinging their dinner buckets, singing, and kicking up dust in gleeful freedom. Their homecoming was the best part of the day. The four of us could then romp through their chores around the farm. I always tagged along with them, learning what I would one day have to do to feed the animals, clean out the barns, or gather vegetables from the kitchen garden.

It was magical, this childhood on the farm. I especially loved all the animals, harboring a deep fondness for the menagerie of cats, dogs, cows and horses that were part of the farm family. There was one pony, named Dick, who became a special friend to me. As the older children were off doing their chores, I was content to spend hours walking him through the pasture, singing to him and chatting with him.

Alas, the day arrived when I, too, had my own chores to do, just like everyone else. I was never happy with these assignments. But that didn't really matter on the farm. Everyone did their bit to get the chores done whether they wanted to or not.

One of my earliest farm chores was riding Dick out to the pasture to bring the cows to the barn. What a perfect arrangement! I could ride him out there to the far corners of the farm where nobody could see us, and we could find all kinds of fun things to occupy us while everyone else was busy doing their things in the barns. Then at the last minute, I would round up those cows and head homeandnobody would bethe wiser.

But the Lord is so often gracious to find ways to expose our waywardness, even when we're young and foolish. One delightful summer evening, as the heat of the day waned and the sun began to move lower in the sky while a breeze gently rustled through the leaves, my pre-chore exploration took me further than expected. An unfamiliar stream, way on the far edge of farm, was simply too alluring to avoid.

We galloped along in exuberant expectance of adventure, Dick and me, listening as the gurgling of the stream moved into earshot. All of a sudden, wary of the unfamiliar territory, Dick planted his feet firmly and came to an abrupt halt. I, of course, did not halt, but continued galloping on, right over Dick's head and into the water. Ever the faithful partner, Dick immediately dashed away to the barn where Father was busy at his evening chores. Knowing Dick's solo return could only mean that something had happened to me, he immediately he mounted Dick and set out to find me, searching across the acres of farmland. When he finally found me, he stopped short and stifled a relieved chuckle.

There I sat in the middle of the stream, embarrassed crocodile tears dripping down my nose. I wasn't hurt, but I knew right away that I had disappointed my dear father. He didn't have to say a word to me; he just lifted me out of the stream and onto Dick's back again. Silently we trotted home. I tried to be more faithful about doing my chores after that.

The social life of a farm girl in the early 1900s consisted of special events at the country school and church and quiet evenings at home with the family. Church suppers occurred frequently, as did student poetry recitations at the one-room school-house. The whole community turned out for these events.

Iowa winters often kept the family housebound, and we found ways to stay busy during the long, snowy evenings. My siblings loved to gather in the warm, toasty kitchen for a taffy pull. We'd each get our own wooden spoon. Mother would get out the sugar and syrup and reveal peppermint she had been hiding for the first snowy night. Oh, the mess we made! It was such fun!

On warm summer nights, we made enough ice cream to fill the whole freezer. Father wanted to make sure we didn't forget our spelling and arithmetic while school was out, so mother would serve us our special treat as dad quizzed us. It was always a competition!

"Spell chrysanthemum, Harold!"

"375 divided by 5, Eleanor!"

"If you answer this correctly, you'll knock Iola out of first place, Mabel! Name the capital city of Illinois."

I rarely won these competitions. I was too busy having fun most of the time and could just could not seem to find the time to do my lessons as I should have done them.

Those were the days—not a care in the world and God's great out-of-doors as a playground!

Mabel's Iowa

"The land yields its harvest;
God, our God, blesses us."
~Psalm 67:6

There is a geography thatimprints itself on our souls. Winemakers call this "terroir:" the the soil that allows the fruit to grow also flavors the wine that comes from that fruit. The fruit of Mabel's life was flavored by Iowa terroir. Despite living in the D.C. region for about 75 years, Mabel's life emanated the flavor of the soil that she was rooted in. Over seven decades of living a thousand miles away could not diminish it. I never realized how much the Iowa imprint was part of Mabel until I visited her native Winterset, IA, to be there among her family when she was returned to that ground.

Mabel always intended for this quiet, rural cemetery, just outside the town square and down the road from the family farm, to be her final resting place. She joined generations of family members there, though of course she did so in typical Mabel style: hers is no doubt the only pink urn upon which the good folks of Winterset have ever turned a spade of dirt. Even after decades of life away, Winterset was imprinted on Mabel's heart. When she made her way east to do her part in the war effort, Mabel transplanted that Iowa heartland into the sometimes disheartening whir of life around the Capitol Beltway. I often wondered where her unwavering optimism and fortitude came from; treading upon her Iowa soil helped me to know and understand Mabel better. A little slice of Iowa heaven was knit into the fabric of all she was and all she would do for the rest of her life.

Iowa in June stretches out in a green and golden grid, interrupted by corners rolling with lush trees, punctuated here and there by a few free

6

form patches of shimmering blue green. Corn undulates in perfect squares, interrupted by the occasional silo and intermittent lonely farmhouse. The face of Iowa, however, hasn't always looked like this. When Mabel lived here, farms were smaller, and there were more of them. Even if several of those grid squares on the map belonged to one family, various family members—sons, daughters, nieces, nephews, grandchildren—would be assigned to a particular plot, live in a house there, and be neighbors.

Winterset sits surrounded by these vast farms and fields. Its Mayberry-esque town square is anchored by the late 19th-century domed City Hall building. Other buildings around the square give an intentional nod to the previous century, such as the restored theatre that opened as a Vaudeville theatre in 1900, which showed "talkies" in 1931. On the south side of the square, there's the Quilt Museum, reminiscent of the society of industrious farm wives and daughters. The 1886 building that houses the Quilt Museum was first a hardware store, and then became H.N. Shaw's dry goods store in 1900. From 1931 on for about the next 60 years, it was the local J.C. Penney. A 1950's ad posted in the museum reflects the spirt of Iowa and the times: "At Penney's we offer no expensive frills such as charge accounts, delivery service, or fancy wrapping."

When I was there for Mabel's burial ceremony, the museum was hosting a "Quilts of Valor" exhibit to honor veterans. The soft artwork hanging on those walls is emblematic of the values woven into the fabric of this community: the value of the work accomplished by our own hands, and gratitude for those who protect our freedom to do that work. These are basic, humble, traditional American values.

It's no surprise then, that just a block away is the John Wayne Birthplace and Museum. John Wayne, of course, is a Hollywood icon and symbol of American values to millions of people. Born in a modest four-room house that would seem claustrophobic to most of us these days, he fell into stardom accidentally in his pursuit of honest work. John Wayne mostly just wanted to treat people the right way because of his conviction that they would then likely do the same for him. He was a contemporary of Mabel Sawhill and came from the same soil.

The north side of the square claims more contemporary fame. It was there, at the Northside Café, that Clint Eastwood and Meryl Streep celebrated their illicit *Bridges of Madison County* love affair. They serve stick-to-your-ribs mid-western fare there, along with the opportunity to sit your rear end on the same bar stool on which Clint Eastwood once perched his derriere.

But there are some tidbits to the story that only local exposure can reveal, and which my bed and breakfast hosts shared with me while I was there. A lovely old Winterset widow had given permission for the cast of the movie to use her beautiful turn-of-the-century Victorian home as the home of Francesca, the main character in the movie. A week before the movie was set to begin filming, however, she discovered the key element in the plot: Francesca's adulterous affair with a photographer who had come to town to shoot the picturesque covered bridges in the area.

"Not in my house!" The widow rescinded her offer to the producer. No doubt Mabel would have said the exact same thing. A sense of rightness and conviction grew in the folks of Winterset just as the corn grew from the soil.

Idyllic though it is, Winterset is not a place of fantasy or disconnect from reality. But this land, this terroir, seems to have instilled a sense of community and interdependence in the folks who live there. Their grid of small family farms put them in inescapable proximity to their neighbors, especially when Mabel was growing up, as I learned from Mabel's nephew Ed, who shared some of his aunt's Winterset history with me. If one farm grew corn and the other grew beans, she had told him, they traded so each family would have they needed. Folks didn't have money to buy things, so they engaged in creative commerce. Disagreements and difficulties happened, as they always do, but they were worked through, albeit noisily, on front porches. Especially during the Depression years, they had no choice but to slog through difficult relations with neighbors, because, well, they needed beans. And there was no escape; there were no big box stores, there were no Amazon orders. They needed each other to fulfill the tasks of their daily existence. Out of this necessity, I think, grew Mabel's instinct to create community among whatever group of people she found herself. Out of the land from which she was raised came the impulse, born of Iowa habit, to be in relation with whomever crossed her path, and to care for them.

The day after her burial, her family invited me to go out to the Sawhill family farm with them. Now owned by a distant relative, the farm no doubt looks different than it did during those days when Mabel "got lost" in the hayfield, coincidentally (she would tell us with a wink) at the same time chores were supposed to be done. The shiny blue silos have nothing to do with the 1920's agriculture, and the barns that are still there house scattered farm equipment rather than living, breathing livestock. The house she was born in is long gone, and much of the soft, gray, weathered wood that covers the remaining outbuildings leans into whatever direction the wind blows.

As I looked out over the quiet farm, trying to figure out where Mabel tumbled head over heels off her beloved horse Dick, Mabel's great-nephew, Sean, tapped my shoulder and showed me a note he had written on his phone: "It's so peaceful, isn't it?" Even though Sean is deaf, he could feel the still and the quiet. If we stood long enough, the gentle goodness of the land could seep up from the dirt and fill our souls.

Perhaps, during those early years of her life, the peace of this place so filled Mabel's soul that it sustained her throughout her life. Perhaps it was the vision of the world embraced by people living a simple farm life and echoed by voices that stubbornly reverberate in 21st century Winterset— the quilt museum that memorializes the craft of doing beautiful work by hand, the John Wayne museum that praises traditional values—that formed her into the 103-year-old legend of D.C. catering fame. Whatever it was, she was irrevocably tethered to this Iowa land and to its ideals. The terroir of Mabel's life was unmistakably Iowa: the simple, enduring values of hard, honest work; intentional investment in community; and abounding, rich gratitude to her Creator.

"The thing of it is," Mabel would say, "people are pretty much the same today as they were back then: we just need God and each other."

Mabel Remembers: Goodbye Farm, Hello Des Moines

For most of us, life's path is strewn with difficult providences. Mabel's life was no different from most others, and she was never shy about sharing her stories with folks. When she walked me back through her past, though, her frequent conclusion to her stories, even challenging ones, was, "I've had a wonderful life."

Her heart swam with gratitude to God, and she wanted to share that with anyone who would listen. No doubt she hoped her gratitude was contagious; she took seriously the command to "tell how much God has done for you" (Luke 8:39).

Mabel embraced the messiness of my life—crushing disappointments, unmet expectations, and broken dreams—with the gentleness and wisdom born, I see now, of some of her own heartaches and trials. That season of life on the farm with the family that she so adored, though idyllic and uncomplicated during Mabel's early childhood, was cut short so that her younger brother, Wilbur, could attend a school for deaf children in the city of Des Moines.

Wilbur, and in later years Wilbur's entire family, were the light of Mabel's life. Knuckle deep in chicken salad for the next day's Sunday brunch at camp, Mabel brimmed with love as she introduced us to her beloved Wilbur.

• ● •

I couldn't have been more thrilled when Wilbur came along. Finally, someone for me to play with who didn't think he knew more than me. Wilbur was a happy boy,

10

always busy doing whatever he could find to do around the farm as a little one. He loved the farm animals, and he constantly pattered around with Mother, just as I used to do, giggling and cheerfully enticing siblings away from their chores and into games of catch or convincing them to help him find interesting bugs. How the four of us loved to dote on him!

With all of us siblings along with the myriad of grownups around the farm, Wilbur needed only to point or make a particular expression to get what he needed. But as he grew a little older, it began to dawn on us that he didn't talk—at all. Finally, Mother's concern persuaded her to consult a doctor. When the older children went off to school, she packed up Wilbur and me for the trip to Des Moines. I'm sure I found some nice folks in the waiting room to keep me company while Mother and Wilbur visited with the doctor. I wondered what we would have for dinner after the long trip home, and if there would be sunlight enough left for playtime around the barns.

They finished their consultation, and we left the office, Wilbur and me hand in hand as we walked down the steps of the big, unfamiliar city building. Mother's usually confident step faltered almost immediately, and I was shocked and bewildered when I looked up to see, for the first time I could ever recall, tears streaming down her strong face.

"Wilbur can't hear." Mother was distraught. Not knowing what else to do, I lifted Wilbur closer to Mother, and laid my hand on her shoulder as she quietly sobbed. Things were going to change. As young as I was, I sensed that certainty.

Our family now faced a difficult decision. Either Wilbur would leave the farm and the family to attend the Iowa School for the Deaf at Council Bluffs, an almost unfathomable 120 miles away, or the family would move to Des Moines and he would attend the School for the Deaf there, about 40 miles away from the family farm.

After much prayer and discussion, my parents decided that the family would move to Des Moines and my father would continue farming in Winterset and join us on the weekends. Although it was at times difficult on the family, we never regretted the decision.

The transition from Winterset farm life and a one-room school-house to Des Moines city life and a big, bustling brick school was culture shock for me. I was going into the sixth grade when we made our move. Everything was strange and different, and I knew I was as different to my new classmates as they were to me. It barely took any time for me to notice that I was the only one in my class who had to wear tennis shoes instead of more fashionable "Mary Janes." "Why can't

I get a pair of real shoes?" I pestered my mother after meeting some new friends whose footwear was much more sophisticated than mine.

She replied matter-of-factly, "We can't afford them." I did not ask again. But never again would I be satisfied with my regular farm clothes. Who knew that way back in the 1920s in Des Moines, Iowa, seeds were being planted that would reap a harvest of fashion-forward leopard print shoes, bags, and dresses that became my trademark for the next 90 years!

During those cold Iowa winters, my mother insisted that I wear long underwear—and yet again, I was the only one in the class who had to. When I rounded the corner on my walk to school and my mother could no longer see me, I yanked those long underwear over my knees so that none of the other kids knew that my old-fashioned, country mother still made me wear long underwear to school. I was determined to make new friends and fit in, and if I had to suffer a little cold to do so, I was willing to do that.

But still, I missed life on the farm. I missed all the animals. And I desperately missed seeing my father every day. Soon, however, I adjusted to life in the city with my mother and siblings and new classmates. By the end of the year I was selected by my principal at Clarkson Grammar School as a student spokesperson to represent my school at the new junior high school which would be opening the following fall. Despite the difficult transition, I did well in my studies that year. The principal even called my mother to tell her that I could skip a grade. My mother decided I should stay in my assigned grade, but I was pleased as punch that the principal had noticed me.

My school years in Des Moines continued smoothly and uneventfully for the most part. I became involved in whatever I could. Although I never neglected my studies, I must admit that my heart was a bit more focused on my ever-expanding social circle. In many ways, I haven't changed much since then.

Wilbur also did well at his new school. In later years, we often mused that the school helped build a foundation for him to be successful in life. He overcame many of the difficulties associated with his hearing deficiency and learned how to navigate through the world quite nicely. Wilbur raised a lovely family and enjoyed a long and wonderful life. We remained the best of friends through all of his days, and although my heart broke in two at his passing, I rejoice that we will be together again in Glory.

• ● •

Her heart did indeed break at Wilbur's death, as it did when each of her other siblings passed. And I have no doubt that there were glorious, joyful reunions when Mabel joined them.

Mabel spoke fondly of this Des Moines house from time to time. It stayed in the family and was a happy gathering place for many years, despite signs of invading deterioration of the surrounding neighborhood. I drove past it after attending her Winterset burial service. The porch now sagged a bit, host to a tattered couch where a small dog perched, wagging its tail and hoping for some attention. No doubt the rusted chain-link fence was not part of Mabel's childhood architecture. Sadly, the house is now worn around the edges, as Mabel had anticipated years ago. I wondered, as I drove by, what it looked like to Mabel then, around 1924, when she left the wide-open grids of swaying corn stalks and soy bean fields and the friendly town square of Winterset, dominated by the shining gold-domed City Hall, for the activity, energy, and noise of the city.

With nine decades of intervening memories framing her recollections, Mabel had the luxury, she often said, of seeing how God is always "working things together for the good of those who love Him" (Romans 8:28). Perhaps Des Moines prepared her for the decades she would spend in the bustle of the D.C. beltway region. And providentially, her residence near D.C. provided further opportunities for the children and grandchildren of her beloved Wilbur to be near her while they were educated at some of the country's best schools for the deaf.

"You never really know everything God is doing with your story," she told me, pouring dressing over spinach and strawberries I had just arranged for her, the chicken salad stowed away in the fridge by now. "It might seem difficult, but He is working in your life, and He is always good. Look at what He has done through this little farm girl from Iowa!"

It was a wonderful life, indeed, Mabel!

Recipes: Appetizers

Mabel's plan for this book about her life included sharing her recipes separated into categories that responded to seasons of her life. Just as her life on the farm set the stage for the rest of her life, so should appetizers set the stage for an occasion. The best appetizers, Mabel said, would be lovely, just as her childhood on the farm was lovely. They would be simple, and they would be satisfying. And as her early life on the farm built foundational principles into her life, so these principles of efficiency, beauty, and simplicity undergirded her entire approach to a decades-long ministry of feeding people.

Fresh Crab Dip

1 lb. lump crab meat (fresh is always best if your budget allows)
1 8 oz. cream cheese, softened
Jar of prepared chili sauce

Drain crab on paper towels and sort through to make sure all shells, bone, etc. have been removed. Combine cream cheese with crab as gently as possible, until cream cheese is smooth and all lumps are gone. Separate into two batches, then roll each batch into a ball. Cover with plastic wrap and refrigerate for at least a couple of hours.

Uncover and put onto a plate. Drizzle with chili sauce. Serve with crackers arranged on the plate around the crab ball.

Serves: 16

Hot Crab Dip

1 lb. crab meat
1 tbsp. horseradish
½ bottle capers, drained
1 tsp. grated lemon rind
2 – 3 tbsp. grated onion

dash of Tabasco sauce
2 c. mayonnaise
¾ c. grated sharp cheddar cheese
dash of Worcestershire sauce

Mix together all ingredients except cheese. Spread into 10-inch pie plate or other similar serving dish. Cover with shredded cheese. Bake at 350 for 20 – 25 minutes until bubbly. Serve with crackers.

Serves: 12

Meatballs

1 5 lb. bag of prepared meatballs
I jar of chili sauce
Grape jelly

Mix the chili sauce and grape jelly together in a bowl. Adjust the amount of grape jelly according to how sweet you prefer the sauce to be. (Usually about ¼ c. seems to please most palates.) Place the meatballs in a slow cooker and pour the chili sauce mixture over them. Cook on low 4-6 hours.

Serves: 12

Rosenfelder Dip

This is a hearty appetizer and is often a favorite among crowds of hungry teenagers. Mabel borrowed and subsequently expanded the recipe from a family at Wallace Church (the Rosenfelders, in case you were wondering) for whom she had deep affection and admiration.

4 lbs. ground beef
1 2 lb. block of Velveeta
1 24 oz. jar of chunky salsa
2 cans Campbell's cheddar cheese soup

In a large industrial size skillet, brown ground beef. Drain fat. Slice Velveeta into one-inch cubes. Add to beef and stir until melted. Stir in salsa and soup. Serve with tortilla chips. (Four large bags.)

Using the amounts above, this recipe has fed groups as large as 50, either as a warm-up to dinner, or as an evening snack after an active and busy day. The recipe can easily be halved, and although we never had leftovers, Mabel said she thought it would freeze well in that unlikely event.

Serves: 24

Spinach Dip

1 package chopped spinach	½ c. chopped green onions
1 c. mayonnaise	1 c. sour cream
2 tbsp. lemon juice	1 tbsp. Salad Supreme seasoning
½ tbsp. dill weed	

Thaw spinach. (Do not cook). Drain well by placing in cheese cloth or a linen towel. Squeeze well to get all water out.

Mix all ingredients together and scoop into serving bowl. Chill 2-3 hours. Serve with fresh vegetables and crackers.

Serves: 8 - 12

Spinach Artichoke Dip

This recipe is a variation of the dip above. It is not a Mabel original, but one that she tried at our house. She loved it so much that she served it as an appetizer at luncheons and wedding receptions.

8 oz. cream cheese, softened
¾ c. nonfat Greek yogurt
2 c. flat leaf spinach
2 tbsp. water
12 oz. artichoke quarters
Optional: 2 French baguettes

1 tsp. onion powder
½ tsp. garlic powder
1 tsp. salt
½ c. shredded mozzarella, divided
¼ c. grated parmesan

Beat cream cheese with an electric mixer until smooth. Add yogurt; continue mixing. Reserve. Place spinach and water in microwave safe bowl; microwave 2 minutes. When cool enough to handle, squeeze to remove excess water. Cool and chop.

Chop artichokes. Fold into cream cheese mixture. Add onion powder, garlic powder, salt, ¼ c. mozzarella and parmesan. At this point, you can put the mixture into a baking dish and top with remaining mozzarella. Bake at 350 for 15-20 minutes, until mixture bubbles and is slightly browned.

For a fancier presentation:
Cut the baguettes in half and remove the bread in the middle. Fill each half with spinach artichoke mixture and sprinkle with remaining mozzarella mixture. Bake at 350 for 15-20 minutes, until mixture bubbles and is slightly browned. Cool, then slice to serve.

Serves: 12

Vegetable Dip

1 pt. sour cream
½ c. mayonnaise
1 tbsp. hot horseradish (or more, to taste)
1 tbsp. paprika
1 tbsp. minced green onion (or scallions)
1 clove minced garlic

1 tsp. salt.
1 tbsp. tarragon vinegar
1 packet Knorr vegetable recipe mix
¼ tsp. black pepper

Mix all together and chill for at least one hour. Serve with sliced raw vegetables. For the most attractive vegetable plate, use a variety of different colored vegetables: carrots, red and yellow peppers, cucumbers, and celery.

Variations:

- To dip, add one 10 oz. package frozen chopped spinach, steamed and squeezed dry in paper towels.
- Serve in a bread bowl: purchase a round rye or sourdough bread loaf. Cut off top 1/3 with a serrated knife. Scoop out bread and tear into pieces to serve along with veggies. Fill bowl with dip.

Serves: 12

Hot Clam Dip

1/4 c. c. chopped green pepper
1 c. shredded cheddar cheese
¼ c. chopped onion

¼ c. chili sauce
¼ c. butter
1 c. minced clams (drained)

Cook and stir onion and green pepper in margarine. Add cheese and cook over low heat, stirring constantly until melted. Add clams and chili sauce and heat through. Transfer to a serving dish and serve hot with crackers.

Serves: 8 - 12

Smoked Salmon Spread

4 oz. smoked salmon (not lox)
8 oz. cream cheese, softened
2 tbsp. snipped fresh dill
2 tbsp. fresh lemon juice
¼ tsp. white pepper or black pepper

dash bottled hot pepper sauce
finely chopped red onions (optional)
capers (optional)
fresh dill sprigs for garnish

In a food processor combine salmon, cream cheese, snipped dill, lemon juice, pepper, and hot pepper sauce. Process until smooth. (This can be made the day before, covered, and chilled.)

Serve with crackers and red onion, capers, and dill sprigs as toppers.

Serves 8 - 12

Creamy Fruit Dip

1 8 oz. package cream cheese, softened
½ c. brown sugar
1 c. sour cream
2 tsp. vanilla

Squeeze of fresh lemon juice
½ tsp. cinnamon
1 c. cold milk
1 pkg. instant vanilla pudding mix

Beat cream cheese until smooth. Mix in brown sugar. Add sour cream, vanilla, lemon juice and cinnamon. Beat until blended. Add milk and pudding mix. Beat gently until well combined.

Chill at least 1 hour. Serve with a fresh fruit tray. (Suggestions for arranging on p. 123)

Serves: 8 - 12

Part Two
Moving On

"Whatever you do work at it with your whole heart, as working for the Lord, not for human masters."
~Colossians 3:23

Mabel Remembers: Off to College

Mabel's industrious, bent fingers were wrist-deep in flour as she to roll out the dough for sticky buns.

"That needs a little more butter," she told Frank as he stirred the brown sugar and butter on the stove—the sticky bun magic. She plopped another loaf of dough on her cutting board and began to roll. On the other side of the table, I stood with my favorite knife, ready to perform my role in the assembly line. After Mabel smeared the rolled-out dough rectangle with the gooey sugar magic, I sliced the roll into one-inch pinwheels, striving to maintain Mabel-approved circle form for each. Teenage campers popped in and out, curious to see how bare loaves of frozen dough and a bit of sugar would become sticky bun heaven for tomorrow's brunch.

There's an art to achieving the perfect sticky bun. Each part of the process needs to be just right. The dough needs to be at the appropriate consistency—thawed but not still a bit firm, so that if you get to the very center of the dough, it might still be a little bit cold. It needs to be firm enough to cut through without the dough collapsing into mushiness. The sugar and butter ratio needs to be correct, starting with amounts close to what the "recipe" calls for and ending with Mabel tossing in of "a little bit more" of one or the other. The magic formula seemed to be the point where the sugar mixture runs off the spoon, but not very easily. It's a little bit like the perfect sand in a child's sandbox: it will make a castle, but not a very study one. At this point, the dough is rolled into a nicely formed rectangle—"you know, about this big," Mabel would say. Just the right amount of the melted brown sugar and butter must be spread to cover the dough generously up to its edges without oozing out and making a mess as we jelly roll the filled dough.

This time, my pinwheels were mushy ovals instead of precise circles.

She didn't mind (much). Mabel always wanted her signature sticky buns to be up to par, but she was far more interested in the conversations that aroseas we worked. She laughed at my frustrated and distracted efforts as I plopped another set of misshapen pinwheels into the pan.

"She'll be okay; it's just going to take a while to make the adjustment." Mabel knew I was worried about our daughter who had recently gone away to college and had been blindsided with fierce homesickness. "It's the perfect place for her," she reassured me, referring to the small Christian college she had chosen to attend. "She'll figure things out and will end up having a great time."

A good time was the farthest thing from my mind at that moment; I was just hoping she would survive the weekend. Reaching for a distraction to ease my anxiety, Mabel recalled her college days at a small Christian school in Missouri.

• ● •

I knew that Tarkio College, a small school in a rural farming community, was the perfect place for me as soon as I visited. Mr. Ralston, a minister and family friend, suggested that it might be an ideal choice for me. And besides, Mother and Dad figured that the school's affiliation with our Presbyterian denomination would keep me out of too much trouble. I felt right at home from the moment I stepped onto campus.

With a school motto such as theirs, however—"Set fire, Tarkio"—I knew there were bound to be some kindred souls who would partake with me of the delights of our newfound freedoms. I was thrilled beyond words at the prospect of this new adventure.

I didn't need much encouragement to get myself involved in all kinds of campus activities. Always the competitor, I was naturally drawn to participating in whatever kind of sporting team was available, although there weren't as many for us girls back then as there are now. Field hockey was my favorite, and I also played basketball, tennis, and volleyball. Of course, just being involved in sports was not enough; I was determined to become a well-rounded young lady. I had made up my mind, therefore, to take advantage of every possible opportunity, so I joined the Women's Glee Club, the Kappa Literary Society, and the YWCA. I was a very active member of the class of 1935.

Providentially, the freshman and sophomore classes of that year enjoyed a particularly lively rivalry, and I enthusiastically joined the amiable fray. Much of our mischief centered on stealing each other's class flag. It became a running contest to determine which class could hang on to its own flag the longest.

The fellows and the ladies, of course, lived in separate buildings, but we knew we needed to join forces if we were to prevail. Eager to make a useful contribution, I determined that the girls' dorm, Marshall Hall, was the perfect place to hang our flag to keep it safe from sophomore thieves. The guys would have to do their part by stealing the flag and finding a way to hand it over to us secretly. Luckily for us, one of the fellows was in charge of cleaning the dorms. He told us about a little-known back entrance to Marshall Hall and arranged for us to be there at an appointed time to receive the stolen flag. He also gave us a rough sketch of the building with instructions directing us to a roof entrance where the flag could be displayed in all its glory. The rest was now up to us ladies; failure was not an option.

Late one night, when we were all supposed to be asleep—there were strictly enforced curfews in those days—I gathered a few brave partners in crime. With our contraband map, we tiptoed up the stairwells. We found a ladder where the fellows suggested it would be and headed through the utility room toward the trap door that led to the roof. Only a handful of adventuresome souls remained with me, the more sensible heading back to the safety of their dorm rooms. The trap door opened easily, and assembly-line style we passed first a chair and then our flag up the ladder and onto the roof. I tied the flag carefully to the back of the chair and posted it proudly to wave in the fall breeze. We returned to our dorm rooms to catch some rest, wanting to be in peak form to appreciate our impending victory.

The next morning, we sat together at breakfast in the Marshall Hall dining room, bleary-eyed after our night's escape, but expectantly awaiting the grateful admiration of our classmates. It wasn't long before we heard the celebratory hoots and hollers coming in through the open windows as the fellows strolled over for their breakfast: our first victory!

Now we needed to guard the flag. Naturally, those of us interested in maintaining our victory needed to take turns cutting classes to ensure that it wouldn't be stolen. Of course, I volunteered. It was a tough assignment, but we were successful, and that flag remained there for days! I may not have been on the way to the Dean's List, but as far as I was concerned, my freshman year was off to a triumphant start!

Fall marched on, and I began to make plans to celebrate my birthday. There was a movie playing in town, and I decided that spending the evening seeing that movie with some friends would be a lovely way to celebrate my first birthday away from home. We needed permission from the Dean to do so, however, because the movie ended past curfew. The older students encouraged me by saying the Dean granted such requests more often than not. My request, however, went unanswered. Brimming with confidence after my leadership in the flag capers, I decided the birthday celebration must go on.

Coincidentally, the fire escape was located outside the window of my third-floor dorm room. All the girls gathered in my room and, one by one, shimmied down that fire escape. Just as I had planned, the fellows met us on the ground to help us down, and we all sauntered into town to the movie theatre. Despite the bewildered looks we received from townspeople who were not accustomed to seeing college students out so late, we had a wonderful evening. Back on campus later that night, we made our way back up the fire escape and crawled into bed, satisfied with our successful scheme.

I was smug in my accomplishment…until I received a call a week later requesting my presence before Dr. Collins, the president of the college. I humbly pleaded my case and repented of the error of my sneaky ways. He was graciously merciful, and life went on.

In order to help with college expenses, I took a job cleaning the second floor of my dorm. It was a great position: it paid $3.50 per week and covered half of my room and board. I always did my work conscientiously, but because I couldn't pass a social opportunity, I occasionally engaged in quick chats with friendly passersby. One day, I took a momentary break to chat with some of my basketball teammates. I perched on the railing of the banister that ran the length of the staircase. The next thing I knew I was flying through the air and landed downstairs on the first floor. I don't know how long I was out, but I came to long enough to hear one of my friends telling the others, "I think Mabel's dead."

"No, I'm not!" I sat up long enough to set the record straight, and then immediately was out again. My friends told me later they called the doctor right away. Thankfully, I had no broken bones and no serious injury; I just had to rest for a couple days.

As soon as I recovered, though, I headed right back out to the basketball court for a game. As if to add insult to injury, within the first couple of plays I tripped over one of my shoelaces and tumbled across the parquet. This time the result was a broken ankle. My father, always the gentle and concerned care-taker, came for a visit to make sure I was on the mend. He even took the x-rays to his trusted family doctor back in Iowa, who confirmed that I would indeed have to spend the rest of that basketball season on the sidelines. As disappointed as I was, I made a point of going to every game and cheering on my teammates with all the gusto I could muster.

• ● •

Back around our metal table in the camp kitchen, trays of sticky buns put aside to rise, we smiled with Mabel, 80 years later, still enjoying the mischievous antics of a college co-ed. She had accomplished her purpose of distracting me, at least for a while.

"You know, you've made prettier sticky buns before," she quipped. "She'll be fine, but why don't you go into town and call her and I'll finish up here?"

Almost immediately, we were out the door, driving into town and up the other side of the mountain to where we could finally get some cell service. There were tears and anguish on the other end of the line, but she was fine eventually and even went on to enjoy her college years. Mabel was pleased when she graduated happily, and with honors.

Six years after that trying weekend, Mabel and I were in Costco, loading a cart full of sparkling water, gourmet cheeses, and puff pastry shells, preparing for the after-church appetizer reception that would be served after my daughter's wedding. She smiled at me. "I told you she'd be fine."

And so will we all be, guided along the way by the God of peace and comfort who reigned over Mabel's long and productive life.

Working as Unto the Lord

"Work…is an indispensable component in a meaningful
human life. It is a supreme gift from God and one
of the main things that gives our lives purpose. But
it must play its proper role, subservient to God."
~Tim Keller, *Every Good Endeavor*

Mabel inspected the kitchen floor at Camp Hemlock, where the church youth group was enjoying their annual Labor Day retreat during one of the last steamy weekends of the summer. Clearly, the most recent Kitchen Patrol team had been negligent in its mopping duties.

"We need to teach them how to use a regular old-fashioned mop. Get them back in here." Orders are orders in Mabel's kitchen. Not willing to risk disobedience, I yelled out for the campers to return, while Mabel turned on her little purple leopard print flats (her choice of practical camp shoe) and stuck a non-mitted hand into the hot oven to check on the status of the sticky buns while she waited for the offenders to return. Her imperviousness to heat always amazed me. Grimacing at the thought of one slight wrong move causing a burn on those old, industrious hands, but knowing that any word of caution was in vain, I rounded up the slackers and brought them in to face the music.

With the dejected moppers back in the mess hall, the mopping lesson commenced. "There's no sense doing something if you're not going to do it right," she admonished the sheepishly downcast crew. After she demonstrated the appropriate mopping technique, she perched on a stool off in the corner, one watchful eye on their work, the other making sure I was adding enough butter to the green beans.

"The thing I hated most about living on the farm when I was growing up," she began, "was all those chores. I wanted to see how far out in the pasture I could make it with my pony, Dick, before the sun went down. If I could make it long enough, I thought, the chores would all be done when I returned. Of course, it rarely worked out well for me. I could never seem to fool Mother and Dad, and usually ended up with extra chores to make up for my sin. Eventually, though, I didn't mind the chores so much. Dick or my other animal friends were decent company."

Now there were some smiles, and the mops sloshed along a little more energetically. Soon the floor was clean, youthful moppers and 100-year-old supervisor momentarily bound as partners in the delight of a job well done as they emptied dirty pails and wrung out the mops in satisfaction.

"See," she smiled at them. "Work isn't so bad."

Certainly, a person who is 100 years old has earned the right to kick back and relax a little. But working hard for so long had become such a part of Mabel's person that it didn't occur to her to stop.

She gave lots of reasons for her remarkable productivity: good DNA, old-fashioned Iowa farm girl habits, her freedom as a single person. And though it may be true that all of these factors contributed to making Mabel into a centenarian worker bee, there is more to it. Once, she wryly confessed to me that she had to keep working to avoid her sinful tendency toward sloth. "Besides," she said, "God doesn't tell me to be warm and filled. He tells me to work."

The truths and commands of Scripture were so etched in Mabel's soul that to do other than they commanded was a foreign concept to her. Though she did not articulate its meaning and implications in the terms of a theological scholar (and how many of us do that, anyways?) her obedience to God's injunction to "fill the earth and subdue it" translated into using her hands, her energy, her resources, her gifts, and her talents to serve others for God's glory. The work she did became a tangible working out of her prayers of praise, a concrete expression of gratitude that overflowed from her heart and hands and onto the plates of the people whom she served.

Her work was an act of culture making—working to bring beauty, order, and joy to a broken world. Mabel's calling and vocation was to take something ordinary God has given to us—food—and make it into something pleasing and delicious, an occasion for joyful communion. She

29

made things beautiful as well; even if paper plates were used, they had to be the right color. And there would be flowers—there must be flowers—to make it lovely.

One warm spring evening, we sat on my patio, enjoying a rare dinner that she allowed me to cook for her, and planning the menu for my older daughter's upcoming bridal shower. She eyed the bed of peonies getting ready to burst into bloom along the wall of the free-standing garage. I saw the wheels beginning to turn.

"What color will those be?" she wanted to know. Those fluffy pink and white blooms became not only the key to our homemade centerpieces, but also the color palette for the food she planned. "No need to spend money on flowers when you've got such pretty ones in your yard," she said. She was also thinking of her pink tiered serving platters for the petit-fours and the frilly white trays she had spied on a ledge in my kitchen earlier.

We created a lovely table. It may or may not have been Pinterest-worthy, though Mabel would not have a clue about that; she neither owned nor ever cared to own a computer. There would be no perfectly composed Instagram shots, but the event Mabel orchestrated was indeed a thing of beauty. There we were in the kitchen, mothers, grandmothers, aunts, sisters, and friends, all busied at Mabel's direction, making things pretty and delicious as we awaited the arrival of the bride-to-be. We had come from upstairs, from the next town, from a state or two away, and ranged in age from 20 to 99.

Together, we were doing the work: we scooped out tomatoes and filled them with shrimp salad (it all fit the color scheme!); we sliced and arranged the fruit; we arranged peonies, baby's breath, and spring roses in mason jars and tied a satin ribbon to hide the stems. We talked and laughed and reminisced about our own bridal showers, 20 or 30 or 50 years in the past, while we each carried out tasks with the common goal of launching the bride joyfully into her married life. Sweeter even than the beauty of the table we prepared was the common purpose that united us: the shared love poured out onto one person on the eve of her new life.

Admittedly, not all the fruits of our labors are delicious, and not all work is fun, festive or successful. Even Mabel sometimes admitted to scorched sticky buns, wilted strawberry spinach salad, or an occasional ungrateful guest at her table. That's the unfortunate nature of work in our post-Garden of Eden world. But still, we too often see our work as merely a necessary part of the process that must be tolerated in order to get to what is really important, good, or fun. Mabel, though, was born into a different perspective, where work was naturally integrated into the rhythms of daily life. On the farm, the day began with chores and a prayer around the breakfast table. Even when she lived on the 8th floor of an apartment building outside of Washington, D.C. instead of on a farm in Iowa, the principle remained the same throughout her many years: just as she woke up and took a breath and put one foot on the floor each morning, so she did the work that had been set out for her to do that day.

She and I checked in with each other every so often to catch up. "Well," she would say, "as usual, when I woke up today, I asked the Lord what He had for me to do today, and I did it." Perhaps there had been a luncheon that day, perhaps she was planning for one tomorrow and wanted to know what I thought about the menu. Often, she had spent time digging through the stash of gifts that she kept piled up in her extra bedroom.

"The pastor's daughter needs this dress," she told me, after she found a frilly little pink tulle skirt with the lace top. It was in a box deep under the table that she hadn't been able to reach until she had given away the box of luncheon dishes with matching soup bowls that had blocked it. Without stopping for a breath, she praised Charlotte's father for all the work he did for our congregation and the wonderful sermon he preached last Sunday, went on to rave about the beautiful manners of all four of the children, and finished with a declaration of how kind their mother is. "Which is why Charlotte needs this dress," she concluded.

The following Sunday after the service, we visited with folks when Mabel felt a slight tug on her bright orange skirt. "Miss Mabel," little Charlotte smiled as she pirouetted, swishing the tulle across the chair with a flourish. The appropriate oohs and aahs ensued, while Charlotte reached her hand up to lead Mabel away. "Will you help me get a bagel? I'm hungry." Off they went hand in hand, each serving the other in her own way.

It was all a part of the work God had given her to do, Mabel told me, to use the talent and treasure that God had given her to benefit others. "It works out quite nicely for me too, a lot of the time," she quipped mischievously. "That nice lady at Nordstrom, I knew she needed someone to talk to. She was going through rough times with her children, and I listened. We became fast friends. It just so happened she offered to begin putting aside nice sale items for me. We take care of each other. And when she's ready, I'll start talking about Jesus."

Whatever the task, Mabel was confident that the work was valuable. It didn't matter if the event for the day was for 20 or 200, or even if there was no event at all. Whatever the case, she believed that almost every day came with something to do that involved ministering to somebody else.

Mabel walked through her days with the wind of soul-joy at her back. It arose from knowing God's purpose for her life deep in her bones. Whatever work she had to do was a conduit of God's grace to a hurting world, a way to extend the hands and feet of Christ to those who are in pain or those who are merely unacquainted with Him.

Work, any kind of work, provides an opportunity to make the world more beautiful, to make things taste better, to make things work better, to make things more peaceful, or to put broken things back together again. Work is a way to love our neighbors.

Unfortunately, contemporary culture doesn't always encourage us to view our work—no matter what kind of work we do—as an enriching, fulfilling, and necessary part of life. Rather than seeing it as a way to exercise dominion over our small part of the world, we sometimes tend to see work as a means to an end: something that will earn us a living, an impressive title, a full bank account. None of those is necessarily bad, but all are incomplete. Tim Keller, a well-known pastor who has written extensively on the topic of work, warns us in his book *Every Good Endeavor*, that the result of viewing work this way is that we lead fragmented, dualistic lives. We rob ourselves of the opportunity to appreciate our work for the transformational power it can have. It's a shame when we trudge through the work that consumes most of our hours, yearning only to make it to Friday, garner an impressive title, or reach retirement.

Although she dug into her work with all her might, Mabel had no problem taking breaks from her work to pay attention to other parts of her life. She fearlessly traveled to snowy Iowa most Christmases to spend the holidays with beloved family, and she jumped at the chance to travel to

Australia when she was in her 90s to watch her nephew, Sean, compete in the Deaf Olympics. But there would be no retirement for Mabel. "There's nothing in the Bible about retirement," she said, "so I'll keep working as long as the Lord keeps me breathing." And she did just that. She had three catering events scheduled the week she passed away in April of 2017 at the age of 103.

Mabel's work was an opportunity for her to spend her days doing something she knew how to do to somehow bless her neighbors. She always insisted that everybody has been gifted with the ability to do something, and they also have the responsibility to do it.

Mabel was not a theologian or philosopher, but she knew the Lord well. Her joyful embrace of the good works God had set before her was rooted in an intuitive, Gospel-drenched understanding of work as good and beautiful. It was an understanding more embraced by folks of her generation than folks in our current entertainment-driven culture. I wistfully envy those simpler days, where community was right there in person in front of you rather than on a screen, and where we often needed to work together simply to put meals on the table. It has never been a perfect world, but perhaps Mabel's world had fewer things to distract her away from doing the kind of good work that serves others.

"The thing of it is," Mabel would say, "I do this work because I love to make people happy. And food makes them happy."

The Vine and the Fig Tree

"In that day each of you will invite his neighbor to sit
under his vine and fig tree, declares the Lord Almighty."
~Zechariah 3:10

We cherished the times Mabel spent with us at our house, especially those times when we could get her out of the kitchen and into a rocking chair on the front porch. Even though we live only a few blocks away from a major thoroughfare, and just a few houses down the other way from railroad tracks, we have created a peaceful little slice of earth. I believe our 100-year-old house and the gardens around it spoke to her of her beloved Iowa just a little bit. A few rocks in the rocking chair eased her out of work mode and into a reflective spirit. Knowing that all these nearby planes, trains, and automobiles were an unwelcome intrusion in my vision for my life and home, she would gently point out all the simple loveliness about it. Although she may have been rebuking me for a lack of gratitude for God's goodness, the rebuke was laced with such love that I never received it as criticism. When the sitting got to be too long for her—relaxation was never her strong suit—we'd stroll through the yard, checking out what herbs she could use for upcoming events, or what flowers she might like to cut for tabletop décor.

"Look at that," she said as she pointed a fig tree while we wandered. "You have a vine and a fig tree! I must be in the new Heaven and the New Earth." She was referring to a passage in the book of Micah that give us a picture of what Earth will be like after Jesus returns:

"They will beat their swords into plowshares
and their spears into pruning hooks.
Nation will not take up sword against nation,
nor will they train for war anymore.
Every man will sit under his own vine
and under his own fig tree,
and no one will make them afraid,
for the Lord Almighty has spoken." (Micah 4:3b-4)

The fig tree was here when we moved in years ago; it is one of ways that Frank knew immediately this was the house the Lord meant for us to have. The grape vine was in the ground before the boxes were unpacked, and it has been producing fruit for most of the twenty years we have lived here. I needed a bit of convincing to actually sign the contract to make this place our home. Frank, on the other hand, had his pen in hand the instant he spied the fig tree. Having grown up in urban Queens, NY, and then living in apartments or town homes, Frank had prayed fervently for his own plot of earth where he could raise his family in security and abundance under his own vine and fig tree. Our 100-year-old cape cod, once the only house for miles around and now in the middle of a bustling and lively suburban neighborhood a mere ½ mile from a major thoroughfare, has been God's gracious and perfect answer to that prayer.

Powerful images of the vine and the fig tree fill the pages of Scripture, many of them, pointing to a place and time of peace, security, and contentment. Some of the most poignant vine and fig tree imagery in all of Scripture is the picture of the land promised to the children of Israel—a land of vines and fig trees. It seems fitting that this is the gift that God gave his children: not a place of leisure and idleness, but a land to work that would bear fruit, where his people could prosper and increase and enjoy the fruit of their labor. In a way that continues to surprise me more than it surprises Frank, this is what God provided for us in our humble little plot of earth.

"Except that I doubt there will be any weeds like that in God's gardens," Mabel said as she pointed a pink manicured hand into the herbs. "It looks like you have a little work to do here."

Her point was well taken. Those of us who look for perfection on Earth will face continual disappointment. Our vine and fig tree are concrete reminders of the "already, but not yet"—the reality that we can see and enjoy bits of eternity here on Earth that foreshadow their ultimate consummation in heaven. Thanks to God's goodness and graciousness, we have our very own vine and fig tree in our very own ground in our own quirky neighborhood outside of Washington, D.C. And much like the Israelites as they stood on the brink of entering their "land flowing with milk and honey," stubbornly refusing to go in because it didn't meet their expectations, I was not as eager as Frank to accept this place as the land God had promised to provide for us. They peered over in Canaan and saw giants instead of a welcoming committee; I looked around my new neighborhood and saw siding that hadn't been power-washed in years and trash cans decorating lawns. Like the Israelites, I succumbed to disappointment for not getting what I thought I should get. After all, they had gone through a tough 40 years, and I had had a few tough years myself. It was time for some easier living. Still, this would work for us for at least a little while, and Frank's vision of a life of peace and security under the vine and the fig tree was admittedly a compelling one.

We don't live too far from the banks of the Potomac River where, centuries earlier, George Washington had a similar vision for his life. In 1784, when he returned to Mount Vernon after the Revolutionary War, he wrote this to the Marquis de Lafayatte: "At length my Dear Marquis I am become a private citizen on the banks of the Potomac, & under the shadow of *my own Vine & my own Fig-tree.*" He had returned to his sanctuary, the horrors of war mostly behind him, to his place of peace and plenty.

Our slice of earth is certainly no Mount Vernon, but consider that Mabel, on the other hand, didn't even have a yard. There was no earth to cultivate to make anything grow. (I think the only thing that grew in Mabel's apartment was the number of new shoes and bags necessary to keep her well-outfitted.) Yet I have no doubt she slept and labored and lived her days under the peace and contentment of her own figurative vine and fig tree. Although I suspect she buried in her heart an ache for the fields, space, and soil of her native Iowa, she willingly accepted as her piece of earth her 8th floor apartment with a view of the Capitol dome off in the distance.

The vine and this fig tree, however, are not merely ornamental; they are also productive. It is a supremely fundamental activity to use what the Lord has given us—whether an estate overlooking the Potomac, an 8th floor urban apartment, or a 100 year-old suburban cape cod—for useful and beautiful ends. When God delivers the mandate in Genesis 1:28 to fill, subdue, and rule the Earth, this is what he means: inhabit whatever sliver you've been given and serve others by making that slice useful and beautiful. What Mabel produced in that tiny little kitchen—I've seen walk-in-closets that are bigger—enabled a thousand different occasions, grand and small, routine and special, to satisfy hungers of both our body and spirit.

We're all given different slices of creation over which to exercise our dominion. The key is to recognize the thing we have been given to do and to do it, whatever it is, that will help to increase beauty, peace, and contentment in our domain. For those who are so inclined and have been given some actual earth, to put our own hands into this dust from which we came and to which we will return and produce something orderly or beautiful or fruitful from it is an immense gift. And it is in this active creation that we can be initiators of community as well, because to keep what we create or make is to waste it. What we produce from the various vines in our small garden or from the fruits of our labors sweetens when shared with community.

Though the domain may be modest—a tiny kitchen in an 8th floor apartment or an unassuming home in an untidy transitional neighborhood—it is no less significant to the God who placed you there than Mount Vernon was to George Washington. My dear husband's vision of his vine and fig tree allows him to embrace our imperfect world gratefully and enthusiastically. In fits and starts, and with much wrangling with God about my unmet expectations, I have come to seek rest under our vine and fig tree as well. Both Mabel and Frank intuitively grasp the vision of their own imperfect homes as a where we can be constantly surprised by the sparks of loveliness that come to us and go out from us when we seek refreshment and purpose under our vine and fig tree.

The occasions when I catch bright, if fleeting, glimpses of Frank's vision for the life under our vine and fig tree allow me to taste the abundant sweetness of the eternal which has broken through into this world. I cherish those moments.

As Frank and I sit under our vine and fig tree, we're grateful that the prosperity and increase is not limited to the fruit that we produce from the ground. Far more significant is the spiritual fruit with roots that reach deep into the soil of this place. The Israelites did not find Utopia when they entered the Promised Land. Amidst the abundance, they also found hardship and disappointment and toil. We, too, have weathered setbacks, defeat, and difficulty here, and no doubt have more of that ahead of us. Consistent with Micah's picture, however, fear does not and never will abide here, because we have imbibed abundantly of God's grace. Nothing is a clearer and more joyous picture of that as those times this house bustles with the return of our grown children and the eight pairs of little feet that now scamper around and testify to some of the most precious increase of all.

The moments with family and friends gathered around our table, enjoying the fruit of our or another's vine, are proof that God is here among us now. The veil has been rent so that we can already partake of eternity, though the fullness of it is yet to be revealed. When that day comes, we will all sit together under our vine and fig tree and enjoy their bounteous and lavish fruit in absolute peace and harmony and contentment. In the meantime, though, we are going to pick some tomatoes and basil for caprese salad on the porch with our neighbors.

"The thing of it is," Mabel would say, "God provides exactly what each of us needs and we just need to be grateful and get busy."

Mabel Remembers: Woodside High School

I met Mabel the year I switched careers and became a teacher. I was in my mid-thirties, with a new family that unexpectedly included two young teenagers along with my widowed husband. The three of them, along with myself and my seven-year-old daughter, had been merging ourselves into a family for the past two years. We had recently committed to enrolling the kids in private school, a decision not all of them were happy about, especially since I would be teaching there. And, just so that no dust would grow under our feet, we moved into a new home, changed church membership, and planned and attended the 40th wedding anniversary of my parents in Western New York. Then 9/11 happened and hit particularly close to our family members living and working in New York City. Our lives were overloaded, and my emotional margin was dwindling day by day. By the time the end of October rolled around that fall, even maintaining survival mode tested me daily. Thanksgiving and a couple days off is not that far away, my new colleagues reassured me as I frantically graded essays in the teacher workroom. Thanksgiving, I thought, and a houseful of out-of-town family and a huge meal to prepare and beds to figure out for all the visitors. My bones felt heavy.

The five of us slid into the pew on Sunday morning just as the announcements were completed and the service was about to begin. The morning had consisted of multiple efforts of increasing volume to rouse a lethargic teen out of bed, indictments concerning the lack of appropriate breakfast food in the cupboards, and one necessary but somewhat painful hair de-tangling session. My eyes met Mabel's across the row as she scanned our unsmiling faces and my sagging shoulders.

"Did you know that I was a teacher, too?" Mabel asked me. We were just getting to know each other; this after-the-service visit would become a sweet routine of ours throughout the coming years. The kids were milling around with groups of their friends, so we had a little time for a pre-lunch chat.

"But, I almost didn't make it through college first. Times were a little tough then."

• • •

It was 1931 when it was time for me to go to college; between my three older siblings, my father had already managed to keep at least one of my child in college for each of the past eight years. That was no mean feat for an Iowa farmer during the Depression. But I was determined to go, and my father, especially, wanted me to have a college education.

I spent the summer before college working various jobs in order to earn some of my tuition money. Babysitting for neighbor children earned me five cents an hour, and checking out customers at the City Market brought in a whopping ten cents an hour. Summer seemed interminable as I anticipated moving on to collegiate life. Finally, I packed the small amount of clothes I had into cardboard boxes—we had no extra money for extras such as luggage—and hopped into the car beside my father. I was certain this would be the best time of my life.

And it was, until the end of my second year, when I received an unexpected letter from my mother explaining that I would have to pack up all my things and come home for good; they would not be able to afford to send me back to college in the fall. Tuition was $75 per semester and room and board was $7 per week. Oh, the devastated tears I cried as I packed up my dorm room, ready to bid farewell to my beloved Tarkio.

My father arrived to take me home for the summer to find me sitting among the boxes, tear-stained and dejected. In what I didn't recognize until years later was a bold and risky step of faith, he put his arm around my shoulder. "Mabel," he said. "Just leave your boxes here. Even if I have to sell part of the farm, you'll come back here in the fall."

What I did realize at that moment, however, was that this education I was getting required significant sacrifice on the part of my parents. I knew, then, without any doubt, that college was not just for me to have a good time, but to focus on my studies so that I could make my family proud. Over seventy decades later, I can still see my father's face and feel the immense gratitude I experienced in that moment for having such a hardworking, generous, Godly man as my father.

Their sacrifice inspired me to make something of myself as I left college. Of course, because options for ladies were limited in 1935, I began to look for teaching positions. I applied at Woodside High School on the outskirts of Des Moines. The school board was made up of three members: Mr. Schlember, Mr. Melson, and Mr. Goode. I went to each of their homes and proceeded to "sell myself," determined earn a return on the investment my parents had so sacrificially made for me. I guess my youthful enthusiasm paid off, and I was hired as a high school math teacher. With a salary of $90 per month, the highest of all my class who had applied for teaching positions, I thought I had hit the big time.

Thus began a seven-year run, and some of the best experiences of my life. It was September 1935 when I arrived at Woodside High School in Des Moines to begin the next chapter of my life. I had the time of my life at college and wasn't looking forward to moving on, to be honest. And I was afraid of what I could expect from some of these students who were barely younger than me. Most of my professors advised me to be strict from the start. But that wasn't my nature. Leaning on my professor's advice and what the way my parents raised me, I was firm, but kind: no late assignments and no disrespect. We worked hard together, and they learned that the work can be satisfying, just like those chores on the farm I tried so hard to avoid.

As I took the time to get to know them better, I grew to love them. I made it a point to become acquainted with their parents, and occasionally stopped by their homes—that was the way communities operated back in that day—or chatted with them at PTA functions. Mrs. Yoder, a delightful and lovable Swedish woman whose son excelled at math, frequently invited me to stop by on my way home for tea and sweet Swedish pastries. While I was still a block away, the warm aroma of fresh-baked apple cake or cream puffs enticed me toward her front door.

"I'll put the tea pot on," Mrs. Yoder would tell me, "and we'll have a little party." Maybe this is where my love of serving sticky buns took root.

Then there was Mrs. Hobson. Her son, Bob, had to drop out of school because of an illness. I stopped by their home once a week to assist him with the schoolwork he was trying to keep up with at home. Mrs. Hobson always put a pot of soup on the stove for us to have while we worked. She knew I liked pea soup, and hers turned out to be my favorite. It was a recipe I tried to recreate when I started cooking for other people, but much to my chagrin, I found few people with as sincere an appreciation for pea soup as I had in those days.

Mrs. Goode, another mother, had a fresh vegetable and flower stand. As a result of a growing friendship with her, as well as my support in helping her son struggle through Algebra, I was kept supplied with fresh veggies for my plate and pretty flowers for my table.

Soon, my students began to trust me more, and they started to approach me with many of their problems. I often arrived at school early so that I could pitch horse shoes or play basketball with whomever was there. It was during these informal times that we had some of our best conversations. Of course, I always tried to win the game we played. One benefit of being a young teacher was that I was in as fine form as they were.

During my last year of teaching at Woodside, our community suffered an epidemic—it was the flu, I think. Sadly, our superintendent was a casualty of that epidemic. Many teachers then had to assume extra duties for which we did not feel prepared or trained. Because I was the new kid on the block, I was drafted to teach the classes nobody else wanted to teach. I found myself teaching an agriculture class, which I could muddle through because I was an Iowa farm girl. But it was not a pretty sight when I had to teach Geometry, the one math class that I struggled with the most. Somehow, I managed to blunder my way through that class; most of my students even passed!

Sports events were always fun events at Woodside. I'll never forget all those hamburgers I fried at the weekly football games. On one occasion, to celebrate the seniors' final game, we decided to serve a dinner instead of the standard football game fare. I enlisted the aid of Mrs. Yoder, who had three lovely daughters to help as well. Our opening menu was creamed chicken on waffles, plus the trimmings. A great time was had by all. I didn't realize it then, but even back in the 1930's God was preparing me for much of the work I would do cooking for folks, even when I was over 100 years old! "For I know the plans I have for you," He tells us in Jeremiah. How blessed I have been to be able to look back over more than ten decades of life and see how all His plans for me unfolded in my life.

I also enjoyed teaching the seniors, and especially advising them. Choosing what to do for "senior skip day" was always a highlight of the year, and a chance for me to once again take part in the delight of youthful mischief.

• ● •

"The first year or so is always the hardest," she said. I knew that she was talking about more than teaching as she glanced over at the group of kids, including the two to whom I had not too long ago become mother when I had married their father. The 18 and 20 years that separated me from them seemed, at times, far too small a space to navigate successfully.

"I was just about to turn 21," she went on, "and I had students who were 18 or 19. The best advice I got was from my education professor at Tarkio College was to 'throw away what you learned in the books and just use your common sense.' It mostly worked."

"You see, God is always working," she reminded me. "And He often does the most work through the most trying circumstances." Our kids wandered over to us, flashing the "feed us or things will get ugly" look, which Mabel immediately recognized. "But right now, He just wants you to feed those kids some lunch."

Recipes: Accompaniments

Although Mabel never minded being the center of attention (like a juicy roast at Christmas or a spiral sliced ham at Easter), she never underestimated the power of a strong accompaniment. A good main dish on its own was only a good dish, but with the right accompaniments, the whole meal could be unforgettable. Although these dishes are not the star of the show, what they add to a meal or an event make it complete, and even memorable.

Strawberry Spinach Salad with Balsamic Vinaigrette Dressing

This is one of Mabel's simplest and most well-loved "recipes." Arrange sliced strawberries on top of the spinach after tossing with dressing for a particularly elegant presentation.

2 ½ lb. bag spinach   4 lbs. of strawberries, sliced

Combine all spinach and strawberries in a 10 qt. bowl and toss. For more color, toss with a point of blueberries. Serve with Balsamic Vinaigrette Dressing.

Serves: 15

Balsamic Vinaigrette Dressing

2 c. brown sugar

1 c. balsamic vinegar
2 c. olive oil

Combine in a Ziploc bag and mix well. Pour over salad just before serving.

- ❖ Mabel dressed her strawberry spinach salad very generously. For the less developed sweet tooth, reduce the amount of sugar to taste and/or reduce the total amount of dressing made. We often used less than the entire bag, and rarely heard a complaint.
- ❖ In the papers Mabel left for me, I found a yellowed sheet with a recipe for this salad, no doubt the recipe she simplified and enlarged. The dressing for the original recipe, using "2 bunches fresh spinach" is as follows:

½ c. sugar   2 tbsp. sesame seeds   ¼ tsp. paprika
1 ½ tsp. minced onion   ¼ tsp. Worcestershire sauce
½ c. vegetable oil   1 tbsp. poppy seeds
¼ c. cider vinegar

Place all ingredients (except oil and vinegar) in blender or food processor until thoroughly mixed and thickened. Slowly pour in oil and vinegar and blend until combined. Drizzle over salad and serve.

Ambrosia Jello Salad

Jello salads are not necessarily the stuff of 21st century menus. For a side dish of sweet nostalgia, though, with a little bit of fruit thrown in, this recipe can't be beat. It works well with ham and has proven time and time again to be a favorite with kids (of all ages!).

2 c. boiling water

1 can pineapple, fruit and juice

2 boxes orange Jello

1 can mandarin oranges (fruit only)

1 12 oz container Cool Whip

1 can fruit cocktail, fruit and juice

Make Jello according to package directions, except using fruit juice where the box calls for cold water. Chill until heavy syrup consistency. Stir in fruit. Gently fold in cool whip. Spoon into a mold or into bowls. Refrigerate until firm.

Serves: 8-12

Asparagus with Lemon Butter

2 lbs. fresh asparagus (woody ends snipped off)
Butter ¼ – ½ c. depending on your taste (and your waist)
Juice of one lemon
Zest of lemon
One bunch of scallions, chopped

Steam asparagus until just tender with a little bit of crunch. It should still be bright green. (Be careful to not overcook until mushy.)

Melt butter; stir in lemon juice. Arrange asparagus on a platter. Just before serving, add lemon butter and top with scallions and lemon zest.

Serves 8 – 12

Roasted Zucchini Spears

This recipe is not a Mabel original, but one that she raved about after having it one time at our house, prepared with zucchini picked fresh from our garden.

4 zucchini, sliced lengthwise into spears   Olive oil to coat
½ c. fresh parmesan cheese   Salt
3-4 tbsp. Italian seasoning   Pepper

Coat zucchini with olive oil. Season with salt and pepper, and toss with Italian season and cheese. Place on a baking rack placed on top of a regular baking sheet. This will keep the zucchini from getting soggy. Roast at 400° for 15 minutes, until slightly browned on the outside.

Roasted Red Potatoes

1 5 lb. bag of red potatoes (the smaller the potatoes, the better)
½ c. canola oil or olive oil
2 envelopes onion soup mix

Wash the potatoes, and cut into quarters (or smaller chunks if potatoes are large). Aim for a relatively uniform size so they cook to the same doneness.

In a large aluminum tray, toss potatoes with canola oil and two packets of onion soup mix. Stir thoroughly so that all the potatoes are coated. Spread them into a single layer in the tray.

Cover with foil, and bake at 400 for approximately 45 minutes, flipping once during cooking. Potatoes should be slightly browned and crisp on the outside, fork tender on the inside.

Serves 12-24

Sauteed Peas with Mushrooms

1 lb. bag of frozen peas
8 oz. sliced mushrooms
4 tbsp butter

Melt butter in a skillet over medium heat. Add mushrooms and saute until tender. Add frozen peas. Season with salt, pepper, and garlic powder. Cover skillet and simmer until peas are tender, about 15 minutes.

Serves: 4-6

Steamed Green Beans with Cashews

1 lb. bag of fresh green beans
6 oz. cashews
4 tbsp butter

Steam green beans until they are bright green. (If they begin to turn olive green, they are likely getting mushy.) Drain water and toss cashews and melted butter over beans. Season to taste with salt and pepper.

Serves: 4-6

Broccoli Apple Salad

1 large head of broccoli, diced (about 4-5 cups, steamed or raw)
3 Gala apples, diced, skin on
1 c. chopped walnuts
Optional: Dijon mustard to taste

Dressing: 1 c. mayonnaise
1/4 c. honey
1 ½ tsp. apple cider vinegar

Whisk together dressing ingredients. In a separate bowl, toss together broccoli, apples and walnuts. Pour dressing over all and toss until evenly coated. Best if refrigerated before serving.

Optional add-ins: golden raisins, dried cranberries, or diced red onions

Serves: 8 - 12

Vegetable Bean Salad

2 16 oz. cans kidney beans, drained
1 12 oz. can of small peas, drained
1 red onion, diced

1 16 oz. can of shoe peg corn, drained
1 c. diced celery
½ c. green pepper, diced

Bring to a boil:

1 tsp. salt	1 c. sugar
1 tsp. pepper	¾ c. white vinegar
½ c. olive oil	

Pour mixture over vegetables and refrigerate a couple of hours or overnight. Serve chilled.

❖ As in many of Mabel's recipes, the amount of sugar can often be reduced without a negative result. ½ c. of sugar in this recipe is more than enough for most palates.

Serves: 8 – 12

Asian Straw Salad

Mabel raved about this simple salad after she had it at a cookout at our house. It met her most important criteria: easy to prepare, easy to double for a large crowd, and appealing to all ages. She told me it would be a perfect recipe for a church luncheon, but unfortunately she went home to the Lord before we were able to try it out on our congregation.

2 pkg. Ramen noodles (placed in boiling water)	Dressing:
2 bunches diced green onions	½ c. oil (of your choice)
1 handful snow peas, diced	¼ c. sugar
1 16 oz. package of prepared broccoli slaw	1/3 c. white vinegar
(cole slaw will work as well as a second choice)	Seasoning packet from Ramen noodles
1 c. salted sunflower seeds	

Mix together boiled and drained noodles with vegetables, slaw and seeds. Mix together the dressing in a lidded jar; shake well. Pour over noodle mixture and toss well to coat. Can be served immediately or after being chilled.

Serves: 8 - 12

Part Three
The Main Event

"Of all the accusations made against Christians, the most terrible
one was uttered by Nietzche when he said that Christians have
no joy...And we must recover the meaning of this great joy."
~Alexander Schmemman, *For the Life of The
World: Sacraments and Orthodoxy*

Working for Joy

"To live well is to work well."
~Thomas Aquinas

I have an antique sewing machine given to me by my dear friend Mary. It's one of those heavy iron Singers that you frequently see in antique shops. The ones you find in the shops, though, often bear incriminating scars of a long and hard life: nicks and gouges, missing parts, rusty pedals or crooked drawers. Despite the evidence of a useful life, however, this sewing machine has been cared for and well-preserved. Like any fine antique, the patina of the wood adds to its beauty, and the grooves worn into the metal plates under the presser foot whisper about the history of the folks whose feet pressed the pedal and whose hands pushed fabric under the needle.

Probably everyone has seen one of these machines: a smooth-grained oak table set on a scrolled iron work stand. If the whole thing is intact, you can flip the table-top over and lift the actual sewing machine out. What I find really outstanding about this sewing machine, however, is not that it is a quaint old machine that shows us how much harder it was for folks in the "old days" to manufacture the everyday things we need. Rather, what is remarkable is the beauty of the tool. People who admire quality craftsmanship still buy these from antique stores today. On top of the graceful and sturdy base that houses the sewing lever sits a tabletop of honey grain oak, flanked on each side by three useful and decorative drawers, each fronted with delicately carved wreath outlined by a string of tiny beads. You just can't find this kind of workmanship anymore. Even individual drawers taken from these machines are sought after to be used as creative do-it-yourself shelves or storage.

The machine that Mary gave me is a bit rare in that it still houses a working sewing machine. It displays a kind of resolute beauty, proclaiming that a beautiful object can be valued not merely for ornament or show, but also for utility. The thing that does the work can be as beautiful as the thing it produces.

The sewing machine is heavy, with elegantly detailed scrollwork of leaves and vines in still bright gold, crimson, and green trailing across the smooth black iron. Similar decoration covers the base of the machine, although many years of use and as many yards of fabric passing under the needle has dulled some of the gold. Beauty and function intersect in this machine, this mass of wood and metal and simple gears and a needle, made to accomplish one of life's most basic tasks—to clothe people. There is beauty even in the most basic, necessary tasks, it tells us.

I can't help but think that Mr. Singer must have had some ideal of beauty that prompted him to make such a useful, common tool into something that is also a piece of art itself. The attentiveness and skill used to build these sewing machine imbues value and dignity into the work that is accomplished through its use and into the creative act that is enabled by it, regardless of the fact that what is being created is an ordinary item necessary for daily life.

It makes me wonder if, in his early 20th century setting, Mr. Singer knew that he was, in his own way, fighting the rising mentality born of the Industrial Revolution that utility and productivity are mankind's highest values. I wonder if he understood work as good and beautiful rather than a necessary and mechanistic process of input and output that too often can lead to ugliness and mediocrity. I wonder if he knew that our work, whatever it is, can become a reflection of the creativity of God.

I worry sometimes that a quest for ultimate efficiency and productivity, though both are good and meaningful aspirations, has left us without an appreciation of beauty for its own sake. Maybe even more significantly, I worry that we rob ourselves of opportunities to practice our artistry or craftsmanship to reflect the creative genius of God. As his image bearers, there is something of this desire in each of us, to be who we were created to be. I can't help but think that God is as pleased with the person who painstakingly painted the vines on Mr. Singer's sewing machine as he is with Michaelangelo painting the Sistine Chapel, or with Frank Lloyd Wright designing beautiful places to live, or with a chef preparing a satisfying meal. Working on this sturdy, beautiful, well-crafted Singer sewing machine elevates and dignifies the task itself. It reminds me that work itself, even such an ordinary task as sewing pieces of fabric together, can be accomplished in a context of beauty: artful tools being used to create items that benefit and provide value for others all while reflecting the creativity of our Creator himself.

God is disappointed, I think, when the mundane tasks that make up the stuff of our everyday lives are merely an aside to vital, abundant, beautiful living. He made us embodied creatures after all, and bodies need to be fed, clothed, and housed. In all of these necessary activities, divinity beckons. We eat because we have to eat, we build homes because we need protection, we clothe ourselves to stay warm. But there is also an aspect of sanctification and a glimpse of divinity in each these activities that goes beyond our mere survival or sustenance.

In his book, *The Hungry Soul,* Leon Kass reminds us that, for example, we do not merely feed as animals do, even though it is as life-sustaining for us as it is for them. There can be beauty and finesse and refinement to this most fundamental endeavor that at times even allows us a glimpse into the eternal. The skill and artistry involved in preparing and presenting a meal is reflective of the creative nature of God, which, in His order of creation, applies to even the activities that must be carried out daily to maintain life.

Just as the beauty of the sewing machine ennobles the task of making clothes, so also can eating satiate a hungry soul. Perhaps because of the often chore-like necessity of eating, we delight in it more keenly when it is carried out with creativity and artistry. And as we glimpse this aspect of the divine character, bodies and souls are nourished simultaneously.

In 1950, Isak Dinesen wrote a little story about the transformative power of feasting to awaken our souls to the divine called "Babette's Feast." In the story, our heroine, Babette is a poor housemaid for two spinster sisters, who hired her as an act of mercy to give her shelter when she escaped the ravages of civil war in her native France in 1871. Daughters of the now deceased pastor who was the spiritual leader of the community, the sisters dedicate their lives to cheerfully performing good works among the needy of their community, while stoically denying themselves anything but the plain fare of "split cod" and "ale and bread soup." Pleasure of any form other than serving others, in this community, is viewed nearly as a sin.

After being in their employ for 12 years, and upon coming unexpectedly into fortune by winning the lottery, Babette begs the sisters to allow her to provide for them and the community a dinner to celebrate the 100th anniversary of their father's birth.

Apprehensively, the sisters graciously consent to the dinner, vowing, along with the rest of the pious community (their father's disciples) to "endure" Babette's provision for them and to refrain, in honor of their devoted maid, from any commentary on the dangerous French culinary excesses Babette is importing for the dinner. When she lays before them with a "Vieve Cliquot 1860" with "Blinis Demidoff" and turtle soup, the group all maintain their vow to keep silent about the needlessly extravagant food. Nonetheless, they find their tongues are loosed, as decades-old resentments and antagonisms give way to goodwill and warmth. The sisters and their guests grow "lighter in weight and lighter of heart the more they ate and drank."

Upon discovering the cost of the dinner, the economically-minded sisters are horrified and indignant that Babette sacrificed her chance at financial independence for their sakes. Babette corrects them, though, and shares that it was not for their sakes but for the sake of her artistry that she served the feast. This sublime experience opens the hearts of the folks from town to a spiritual reality made concrete. Babette's artfully executed feast set the table for the guests to taste of grace and reconciliation. This once ascetic and sour community is reknit in an expression of joyful piety and gratitude unleashed by Babette's artistry.

I don't know of any occasions when Mabel served turtle soup, and she did not often import fine French wine, yet she infused every one of her events with her own artistry. Even for paper product kind of events, the paper products needed to be of high quality and color-coordinated. And most times, a centerpiece would be required as well. Fruit trays provided by her niece Doreen were so artfully assembled with arrangement of pineapple, berries, and melon that the first people in the buffet line would invariably pass by because they did not want to disturb the composition. Whenever possible, though, Mabel would bring out some of her own serving pieces to adorn the table; it would not be unusual for her to use her beloved Waterford as the centerpiece for even the most ordinary church potluck. Like the worker who carefully brushed the gold leaf onto Mr.

Singer's sewing machines, Mabel infused loveliness into her events because doing something well and beautifully is itself an act of worship. Her life testified that once a person imbibes the beauty of God, she can't help but pour out that beauty into whatever work is set before her to do.

"The thing of it is," Mabel would say, "God is beautiful, so we should make things beautiful too."

Mabel Remembers: Days at Camp Hemlock

Once we had been tapped to join Mabel's crew of kitchen workers at regular church functions, Frank and I knew it was only a matter of time until she would offer to us the opportunity to spend our Labor Day holiday weekend in the famous Camp Hemlock kitchen. Each time the conversation turned to this time-honored tradition of our church congregation, I slipped out of the room, generously (I assured myself) leaving space for others to reap the rewards of working alongside our marvelous Mabel. Besides, the school year had begun, and the rigors of camp life would likely preclude me being at my teacher best on Tuesday morning. But she was on to me, and to resist Mabel was futile anyways. Soon, we were in Labor Day getaway traffic on I-66 West headed toward West Virginia.

We weren't long into our trip when the dreaded red brake lights appeared ahead of us. Not known for his patience in traffic, Frank headed off the highway, confident that the quirky early model GPS mounted to the windshield would find us an alternate route. The monotonous scenery of the highway was replaced by the open expanse of farmland and picturesque one-block towns. A left turn mandated by GPS lead us onto a gravel road, past a white clapboard church, past a cow pasture on one side and a corn field on the other. Mabel and I were thoroughly enjoying the scenery. "Wardensville isn't much different than these towns," she said, preparing us for what we would find when we would finally arrive.

"Remind me how long you have been coming to Hemlock for the Labor Day Retreat, Mabs."

"Well, the thing of it is, I've been coming since the beginning. It has to be about 50 years by now." She looked off into the distance, and I knew I was about to be treated to one of her stories.

• ● •

Around 1960, a group of men from Wallace had a vision for winning and training boys for Christ. They got together and purchased forty acres of land in the mountains a few miles outside of Wardensville, WV. Everyone agreed that it was a beautiful spot, surrounded by all these tall trees and the little brook winding its way down the side of the mountain. You'll see it: we'll drive across it right at the entrance to camp. Most of the important things have not changed a whole lot over the fifty or so years I have been coming here to cook.

At first, the boys camped under that big old Hemlock tree down where the sports field is now. That's how the camp got its name. There was a swimming hole to keep them cool, nothing like the fancy in-ground pool we have today. The vision of the men who began the camp was simple—a place to teach kids the goodness of God's great creation. They wanted to be responsible stewards of that land and their resources and to train kids to catch that vision as well. The main building, that big green one with the fireplace that the kids meet in, was built on foundations which were dug by hand with materials that were salvaged from structures being demolished for "urban renewal" in D.C. The mismatched casement windows and restaurant-style plate glass doors into the lodge came from a D.C. diner that closed in 1960. For years this was the only building in the camp besides the cabins. The long front porch was added in 1962 so that campers would have a place to look out into the forest and stay dry during those infamous West Virginia summer thunderstorms. The addition of the dining hall and kitchen came quite a bit later. Now when we prepare meals for campers, we have the use of three ovens, a griddle, a couple freezers and a walk-in fridge. It's luxurious compared to those early days.

The best part of the whole weekend (besides the food, of course) is the hike up the mountain and the Sunday morning worship up there. There's a path behind the camp buildings that leads to the steep trail. It winds up, up, up through the woods until finally the trail breaks through to an outcropping of rocks. Once they get up there, campers are rewarded with a breathtaking vista that rolls through the hills for miles across the Shenandoah Valley. The sturdier hikers carry guitars strapped to their backs for their mountaintop music. Kids find a rock to sit and they have a Sunday morning worship service together up there on the mountain.

The first year that I was here, however, the paths were not so well worn and familiar as they are now. I had prepared the evening meal with Ruth Bynum, my trusted and capable kitchen partner in those early years at camp. We were ready to begin serving on schedule, but the group had not returned down the mountain. As our dinner growing cold, I found myself frustrated with their apparent lack of consideration in following the schedule, but as the sun was sinking lower in the sky, we began to grow anxious. With only a little time before sunset, we decided we needed to get ourselves into town and track down some folks who could help us organize a search party. Just as we were getting into our car and the sun was disappearing over the western horizon, the first couple of bedraggled campers emerge from among the trees.

Famished, thirsty, and weary, they were grateful for the dinner that was waiting for them. They had gotten lost on the mountaintop, they told us. The path that they thought would lead them down to camp had merely led to a dirt road and an open field. Realizing that the sun would soon be going down and they didn't have time to re-trace their steps back up to where they had held their worship service, they all knelt down together on the pine needle-strewn path and prayed for God to show them the way down the mountain. Together, older ones looking out for younger ones, and making sure that none would fall behind, they began to follow the leaders through the forest again. The Lord heard their cry and brought them safely down the mountain and back to camp. What a good God we serve!

• • •

We were back on pavement now, but GPS was continuing to direct us through the Virginia countryside and away from the clogged interstate. Pink streaks were invading the blue summer sky as the sun blazed lower toward the skyline, and frustrated sighs came front the front seats of the car.

"Don't worry," Mabel assured us. "We'll still get there a lot faster than we used to. When I first started coming here, none of these highways even existed." With the mountains coming closer into view, Mabel mused about all the folks over the years who have poured themselves into the work being carried on at Hemlock: speakers, counselors, organizers, cooks, all bound together by a love for the Gospel. "And don't worry," she added. "The thing of it is…we always have a good time, no matter what."

• • •

Bryan and Kathy Austin were some of the best "Hemlockers" ever. One year when they were in charge of the weekend, we decided to plan for a surprise luau. To effectively pull it off and keep it a surprise, we had to do quite a bit of rearranging to the usual sequence of camp events. We wanted the event to take place at dusk so we could put up lights all around the table. Bryan called the campers around and told them they would have a snack now and would eat dinner a bit later because Mabel wasn't feeling well and needed a bit more time to fix the meal. I sat in the kitchen moaning and groaning with a bottle of ginger ale beside me. Looking back, I see it was a poor excuse. I never get sick!

Anyways, Calvin Smith came into the kitchen to check on me. With his arms around me, he said, "Mabel, just tell me what to do."

I had to throw him off track. "I'll be okay in a bit; I just need to sit here by myself for a few more minutes."

They all left me alone to "recover" and we sprang into action, bringing the luau to life as planned. With bright lights, Hawaiian decorations, and delicious food, we all had a good time celebrating under the stars. Out there, without the lights and sounds of civilization invading upon our thoughts, it is easy to see and feel the wonder and the splendor of our good God.

God is great and majestic like that big, starry, West Virginia sky, but He has a sense of humor, too. And at Hemlock, we want the kids to know the "whole counsel of God," so we celebrate His humor with skit night. Campers are in a flurry all afternoon, sifting through haphazard boxes of props and costumes that have accumulated in one of the lodge closets over the years, pooling their collective creativity as they delight in finding ways to get to that deep, laugh from your gut kind of humor that they'll remember years down the road. Often, I see kids in new and interesting light on this night, when they have the freedom to be a different person in a skit. I have awoken to prepare Sunday brunch many times with aching sides from having laughed so much the night before.

After the skits, they head out to the firepit for the weekend finale, the big bonfire. It's one of my favorite things that happens at camp. With flames reaching toward the stars shining in the black sky, young voices sing praises to God, and many hearts and lives are touched; some are even changed forever. And that's why I come to camp every year.

Sunday brunch has been a traditional favorite of mine; for the kids as well, they tell me. We have ham, bacon, fried potatoes, waffles, egg soufflé, and a beautiful fruit salad. It's a great meal to get them energized for their hike up the mountain. Sunday evening suppers of barbecued ribs are finished with my signature baked Alaska. There's really no "camp food" here. I feed them well because I want them to feel special. Before we leave around noon on Monday, we finish all the leftovers before cleaning the camp and heading home. Many campers have told me this is their favorite meal: they get to remember the entire weekend by sampling little portions of each one before the trip home.

• ● •

We were dipping down the hill and around the curve that empties into town, and Mabel directed us to pull into the Ka-Ka-Pon restaurant, as she and others had done for decades, to enjoy a restful meal before we began our work at camp. I glanced a bit uneasily down at the bag at my feet, stuffed with essays to be graded and assignments to review at some point between meals during the weekend. But Mabel's enthusiasm was infectious; she had prepared us well and we knew what to expect from each day of camp and were prepared to do what we needed to do. What we couldn't know then, of course, was just how precious those memories would be to us in the years after she was gone from us. What I didn't know then is that during each of these 15 or so summer weekends in a humble camp in the mountains of West Virginia, as we rolled sticky buns and scooped hot fudge sauce and cooked barbecued ribs, a little part of Mabel's heart began to beat together with mine. That continues, now that she is gone. It beats differently, of course—nobody can ever fill Mabel's shoes. It beats with gratitude that I had some time to walk alongside side this extraordinary venerable old saint and to watch her live out an abiding century old faith. Now when summer is winding down and my bag is once again full of summer essays to grade and assignments to write, I look forward to another holiday weekend where the hemlocks grow, confident that a camp full of teenagers will be fed, body and soul.

Mabel Remembers: 9/11

9/11 memories for D.C. area folks are framed in spirals of smoke rising from the Pentagon and across the Potomac, followed by an afternoon of epic traffic snarled in all directions away from the city. As most of us sat in that traffic trying to put distance between us and the terror of that morning, however, 87-year-old Mabel, her car stocked full with food, pointed her car boldly in the direction of those flames. She had come to this city over half a century ago to serve her country, and she believed she had another opportunity to do so this day. We had recently met Mabel, and therefore had little exposure to 87 year-olds driving towards burning buildings in the face of a terrorist attack. When we saw her the following Sunday at church, she was anxious to hear how I fared that day, about a week into this daunting new teaching career I had chosen.

I was sitting at a computer at 8:45 that morning, wondering how I would engage a room full of 17 year-olds in a conversation about John Milton's right to "justify the ways of God to Man" in *Paradise Lost*. They were far more intimidating than the lawyers and consultants I had dealt with for the previous ten years of my career.

Mabel nodded understandingly, her mind traveling back through the decades to her own time as a teacher.

"It's not so much about what you're teaching as it is getting them to know that you care that they are learning something. It wasn't a whole lot different seventy years ago when I had a room full of teenagers facing me in a little country school in Iowa. You just have to step out in faith and start doing it. God will meet you and take you the rest of the way. Now help me with these trays of sticky buns." She was satisfied that she had solved my problem, and the trays in the narthex needed to be refilled.

Back in the kitchen, we both recalled the beautiful, sharp blue

September morning. I quickly planned to take my students outside to distract them, when the emergency news banner began to flash across the bottom of my computer screen. Something about an airplane and a building in New York City. I switched to the news coverage and saw smoke billowing out of the Twin Towers. Confused people running down the streets of Manhattan. Another plane smashing into another tower. Other teachers gathered around the screen with me, trying to figure out what was happening. We watched in horror as the Pentagon, 15 miles down the road from us, burst into flames. And as I headed to my 10:00 class, terror in the streets of New York as massive buildings began to collapse.

I had the time it took me to walk down the hallway to my class that morning to plan one of the most critical lessons of my career, one that, as Mabel had predicted, had little to do with any textbook. John Milton was not even on my radar screen as I, along with my colleagues, fumbled through classes as we ourselves tried to wrap our minds around the reality that our country was under attack by terrorists.

"How many events did you have to cancel this week, Mabel," I asked.

"Well, let me tell you a little something…"

• ● •

It was a beautiful late summer morning. I was up early as usual, this time preparing for a busy day with multiple events: my monthly luncheon for the ladies at the Bethesda Women's Club, followed later by dinner for a large group of Navy Officers at the Yacht Club down on the waterfront. I was up to my elbows in chicken salad and beef brisket and didn't bother to even turn on a radio or television that morning. I went about my business, packing strawberry spinach salad, chicken salad, and sticky buns into my cart to wheel down to my car in the garage, oblivious to the terror that had struck just a few miles from my home. If I had even gone out on my balcony, I could probably have seen the smoke rising from the Pentagon. I began to sense something amiss when I pulled into the usually crowded parking lot at the Bethesda Women's Club and had my pick of spaces. Only a few ladies were there, and I knew the instant I saw the look on their faces that something horrendous had happened. We sat in shocked silence, holding onto one another's hands, as we watched the news coverage and tried to eat some of the food I had prepared. Nobody was hungry.

We packed up the leftovers and sent each other home with solemn hugs. The

Lord's special purpose for my day was beginning to stir in my heart as I drove home. I realized then that I would have to make some decisions regarding what to do about the rest of the day. It didn't occur to me when I arrived home to stop preparing for the dinner that was scheduled for that evening. I felt compelled to continue working, even as I continued to watch the horror unfold on television. According to the local stations, there was a ban on all but emergency vehicles on D.C. roads. Still, my heart told me there was a need for this food, but what I wasn't quite sure exactly what I do could with it? I called the Commodore at the Yacht Club.

"What should I do?" I asked.

"Whatever you want to do," was his very unhelpful reply.

So—I prayed.

The Lord gave me the "go-ahead" and I packed the car and started driving to the Yacht Club in downtown Washington, D.C., all the way preparing my speech for the police who would certainly stop me for traveling. I made it to 13th and G Street, where a distracted police officer directed me to go to the left but appeared too busy to stop me. The roads were eerily empty as I made the left and worked my way over to 9th Street, then turned right and into the Yacht Club parking lot. I saw no more police, no pedestrians, no cars; it was surreal. Deserted D.C. streets, I think, can make the most stout-hearted among us feel uneasy. How glad I was to see the Commodore waiting for me at the front door.

"I knew you'd make it," he said, giving me a hug. "You've got guts, Mabel! And can you have the food ready in thirty minutes? We're going to bring in 25 police and firemen. At 7, we'll bring in the other 25."

Anyone who had made it to the Yacht Club that day flew into the kitchen to help get the food ready to feed our first responders at the Pentagon across the river. The Commodore and the two Captains set the kitchen buzzing when they strode through the swinging kitchen doors looking for aprons and serving mits. That day, we all became family in the face of the evil that attacked us across our beloved Potomac.

My mind flew from one quick cooking lesson to the next. Of course, I had no recipes for my spontaneous kitchen staff to follow. I rarely use them. But we were all working in top order; I gave instructions once and saw them followed immediately. Green beans were steaming, red potatoes were roasting, salad was being assembled, beef brisket was warming in the oven.

We brought out the food that had been intended for the Bethesda ladies as well, hoping that we would be able to adequately feed any and all who came through the door hungry. There was fruit, hot chicken salad, strawberry spinach salad, and, of course, trays of sticky buns.

We worked like a team who had known each other forever, and in less than an hour, we had enough food ready to begin feeding the first round of first responders. Some of them came from across the river on boats, some came in their cars; all came for a respite from the nightmarish chaos. They were stunned; they were ravenous; they were grateful. I wished I had more beef brisket; that was the most popular dish for these hard-working public servants.

But they were grateful just to be fed and to rest briefly. They walked through our doors with eyes heavily with sorrow, struggling to apprehend the reality of the carnage from which they had just come. There were no strangers in that room; shock, grief, and anger bound us all together as we grasped at any flickers of hope we could find among us.

I fell into my bed that night, grateful to have been used by God for such a time as this. In my exhaustion I wept for the evil that had burst into flames on this day, but I found solace in my unshakeable confidence that our God would bring beauty out of the ashes of the Pentagon, the World Trade Center, and the field in Pennsylvania. And I slept soundly, as usual.

• ● •

I have little recollection of what I actually said to my students when I walked into class around 10:00 that morning. One student reached out instinctively to hold my hand, almost as if she needed a little help to hold herself up. As the world shook and the smoke rose mere miles away around the Beltway, these kids intuitively moved together into a group at the front of the room, near me, seeking comfort in each other's nearness. Their fear, their concern, their compassion, needed a concrete form; it needed to be turned into some kind of action, even if one as small as an arm on a shoulder. Mabel's instinct on that day was the same. The love she had for suffering humanity required physical expression: hands that made food to feed weary bodies. Even in tragedy, maybe especially in tragedy, this fusion of body and spirit becomes manifest, and compels an 87-year-old to drive through a blockaded city to serve her beef brisket to rescue workers.

Feasting As An Act of War

"Courage, dear heart."
~C.S. Lewis, *The Voyage of the Dawn Treader*

In *The Lion, the Witch, and the Wardrobe,* a beloved children's book, the feasting of the animals plays a significant role. In a particularly memorable scene, the animals are merrily enjoying an abundant feast provided for them by Father Christmas, whose return to Narnia amidst the thawing snow signals that Aslan, the Great Lion, is once again on the move. In joyful anticipation of Aslan's return to their forsaken Narnia, the animals bask in the beauty of the decorations of holly and the sweetness of the plum pudding which he gave them. Their feast, however, is a grave affront to the reign of the White Witch because it represents a threat to her; it tells her that the animals' loyalty lies not with her, but instead with Aslan.

Although I've read this beloved classic nearly a zillion times, it didn't occur to me that the woodland revelry signified something deeper than the happiness we all experience when celebrating holidays among loved ones, or the irrepressible lightness we feel when the last of the winter snow melts away and the daffodil stems strain through the dirt and toward the warming sun. If the Narnian feast had been something so innocuous, the White Witch would not have waved her evil wand to end the merriment forever by turning the animals to stone. No, their feast was something much more. Author and blogger Kelly Keller, when reflecting upon the Yuletide feast in the forest, says that their celebration was no less than an act of treason, a declaration of war.

On the day that our nation was attacked by terrorists, 87-year-old Mabel declared a similar act of war by providing a feast of sorts. With a fridge full of food that had been intended for a celebration dinner that was now canceled as the entire city of D.C. shut down in the wake of the attacks, Mabel followed her instinct for action. With barely a thought, she filled the trunk of her Buick with all the food she had prepared and drove right past the "no traffic allowed" lines towards the smoldering hole in the side of the Pentagon. Although the meal would no longer be savored in peace while watching sailboats drift down the river, it became a feast of another kind: an exhibition of the compassion and brotherhood that lies deep within the human spirit, the kind that is jolted awake in the face of tragedy.

Mabel's meal that day was nothing less than an act of war, a bold declaration against evil and an affirmation of the collective courage to stare in its ugly face and declare that although the destructive forces of evil may sometimes sneer in apparent triumph, and sometimes battles are lost, the ultimate war has already been won for us. Evil loses. Hope wins. Even amidst the rubble, the smoldering ashes, and the mournful cries for lost loved ones, hope lives in the knowledge of that triumph.

And so there was nothing else for Mabel or anyone else to do but continue—to eat, to hydrate, to keep the body going so that it can go into the wreckage to find the survivors, to mourn the victims, and to do whatever the next thing is that we have to do on the next day. On September 11, 2001, she transformed the kitchen of a yacht club into a battlefield kitchen where soldiers could come to be replenished for duty.

The act of feasting is an affirmation of life. In the Bible, all manner of feasts mark significant moments, milestones, and memories. The most glorious celebration of all is a supper—the marriage supper of the Lamb where all who partake will be blessed. Jesus chose a feast, in fact, as the setting for the first miracle of his public ministry: the wedding in Cana, when He turned the water into wine. Abraham commemorated his son Isaac's passage out of infancy with a great feast when the child was weaned. The return of the prodigal son was celebrated with the feast of the fattened calf. The feast of unleavened bread is a remembrance of God's provision of manna for his people in the desert after he led them out of slavery in Egypt. In Leviticus, God commands his people to celebrate the Feast of Weeks in the fall in gratitude for the abundance of the harvest provided by God's providence. Every feast, every celebration, points to something good that the Lord has provided. It makes a statement of God's sovereignty over the affairs of men, his reassurance to us that he is the giver and sustainer of our physical lives. Every feast, then, is an act of war against anything that wants to usurp His authority in the Universe. Much like the White Witch's interpretation of the animals' feast as an act of treason against her authority, Mabel's feast for the first responders on 9/11 was an acknowledgement that the God of the Universe still has authority over evil, even if it may temporarily sink its destructive fangs into creation.

These persistent feasts refuse to give in to the temporary defeat of a long winter or an evil deed. These feasters are fighters, strengthened in battle by knowledge that this world we inhabit, though it is sometimes buried under an ash heap of hate, is a fallen creation that will one day be resurrected, fully redeemed, and inhabited with these same bodies we inhabit now. But these new bodies will be perfect, and unblemished, and indestructible. Can I have an Amen! How can we not continue to celebrate! One of the boldest declarations we can make against evil is to care for our physical bodies even when we're under assault, to soldier on in the supreme hope and confidence of the ultimate outcome.

We often mistakenly assume that to do great things we must do difficult, important, notable things. Mabel's life disproves that theory. Mabel merely did what the Lord gave her to do that day. She often quipped about the early morning conversations she had with Him, wondering what He had in store for her that day. Always, the conversations were rooted in eager anticipation and framed by willing obedience.

I treasured the catch-up phone conversations we'd have every so often. We'd begin by sharing the current day. "Well," she said, "when I got up, I just asked the Lord, 'What do you have for me to do today?'" Often, her day already included a catering slot, but if not, she waited and listened for opportunities to do something for somebody.

In the early morning of September 11, 2001, that daily prayer prepared her heart for a change of plans. While it may have been a remarkable feat for many 87-year-olds to load up a car with food, head into a city reeling from terror from which most people were fleeing, and serve that food to the heroes coming from the ash heap of destruction, for Mabel it was mere obedience. Dear, tiny, fierce, gentle Mabel just went about the work that she and God had talked about that morning.

What is so strikingly convicting about Mabel's life was not her outstanding talent. Her food was delicious, but she would not likely have been the next Iron Chef. What was remarkable about Mabel was that she did ordinary things with extraordinary energy and joy. She taught me that what God requires of us does not necessarily require outstanding talent or gifts. But it usually requires fortitude; it always requires love.

At the feast in the woods of Narnia, one of the little squirrels was so excited about Aslan's impending return that it "lost its head completely." Even in the presence of the White Witch whose wand wielded spells that turned all enemies immediately to stone, he could not help but beat his little spoon excitedly on the table, affirming to the wicked Queen of Narnia that Aslan was on the move. He couldn't contain his joy. So it was with Mabel. Every event she catered, every feast she served was a burst of joyful rebellion against darkness. Every spinach salad, every roasted brisket was a confirmation of the beauty and goodness of this physical creation we have been given.

We should be more like Mabel; we should revel in every feast. Because each time we do, evil shrinks, and another battle is won.

"The thing of it is," Mabel would say, "God has already won the War for us. We just need to keep fighting the battles."

The Heart of Hospitality

"Hospitality is not a house inspection, it's friendship."
~Rosaria Champagne Butterfield, *The
Gospel Comes with a House Key*

An unfortunate result of our social media-saturated culture is that it has transformed the art of hospitality into entertaining—which is decidedly not the same thing—and has consequently scared some folks away from practicing hospitality. Too often, instead of ministering to ourselves and others by welcoming them into our own imperfection, we feel that we need to put our best foot forward (or at least a really good one) before we can open our homes and lives to others. As a result, we end up missing out.

Mabel's ministry of hospitality grew partly out of a need; she wanted to help put her family members' children through Christian school. It continued largely because of her deep conviction that she needed to always keep her hands busy with the work the Lord gave her to do. She also loved to serve and be with folks. Just like many of us, she served well, but certainly not perfectly—she could be a champ at taking advantage of the opportunity to name drop here or there, and she didn't shy away from taking a figurative bow at the end of a well-executed event. Still, her desire to be hospitable was not marred by aspirations of perfection. She wanted food to be prepared well because doing things excellently reflects the character of God; she wanted to make her table delicious and pretty so that the people she was serving would feel honored and valued.

Her family Thanksgivings were legendary. Every year, friends and relatives would come from all over the country to descend upon her two-bedroom 8th floor apartment. In that tiny kitchen, she mixed, stirred, and roasted her way to another holiday of sweet, memory-creating fellowship for family and friends. "Thanksgiving is my favorite holiday," she said, "because I get to tell everybody how grateful I am to God for my wonderful life." While Thanksgiving certainly offered her a perfect platform to do so, she didn't need a holiday to tell folks that, and, being the party-lover that she was, she took advantage of any occasion to get together with folks she loved.

Not one to ever miss out on any occasion for celebration, she switched immediately into Christmas mode for another party the very next day. A sink full of dirty dishes and turkey leftovers notwithstanding, the festivities must go on. Before her family and friends hopped into their respective cars, planes, or trains and headed for their own corner of the country, Mabel would see to it that their Yuletide season began on Black Friday. From somewhere in her apartment, she would haul out her stash of Lenox Christmas china; Christmas treats mustn't be served on just any old platter, mind you. The gold serving cart in the corner, usually storage for various other serving pieces, would be cleared to house the Lenox punch bowl.

If indeed it is true that it is more blessed to give than to receive, Mabel was one of the most blessed people I have ever known. At her "Black Friday Christmas" party, she gave gifts to every single person, each chosen for the specific individual. She started a running list in January, and always kept an eye out for the perfect gift for each person. Somebody half her age could get exhausted with such activity, but Mabel refused to give in to weariness and fatigue, and insisted on opening her heart and home to others, with reckless generosity. The sweet fellowship shared around her table, I imagine, emboldened many hearts toward a vision of perfect, joyous fellowship at a grand eternal feast.

One Sunday not long after Mabel went to be with the Lord, her favorite young pastor, Stephen Coleman, preached a sermon about Biblical hospitality. His sermon, which no doubt Mabel would have loved, was a reminder that although breaking bread together is indeed an important element of fellowship, the most important glorious hospitality happens at the Supper of the Lamb: communion. Around the communion table, we experience the presence of God alongside the multitudes of believers across the globe and across millennia who together make up the faith community and encounter authentic hospitality. To understand it, Pastor Coleman told us, we need to travel back to first-century Palestine. In the absence of restaurants and luxury homes, hospitality was not about haute cuisine and keeping up with the Joneses; it was instead a way to satisfy a genuine need—for food and shelter—in the context of community. There were no McDonald's; there were very few inns. These needs for food and shelter drove folks to community. Travelers sought safety and rest in people's homes, where preparing and sharing a meal with the sojourners essentially invited them into the family. Precious resources were shared. There was no running to Safeway for some ready-made appetizers while throwing a couple burgers on the grill (although I will never knock ready-made anything: Costco delicacies have more than once furnished the table for the most worthy of gatherings, Mabel's included). Throughout most of history, however, meals did not often materialize out of abundance, but came from the family's daily bread. How precious it is to share from what is needed, rather than from excess.

The culture of first-century Palestine dictated that the host offer not only food and drink to his guest, but that he also extend the same physical protection he would offer his own family members. Under the oppressive thumb of the Roman Empire, there was a real threat that harboring the wrong kind of person, Christians especially, could lead to imprisonment. Heads on platters really happened, frequently, and far more often than most of our 21st century American psyches care to comprehend. The head of the hosting household was honor-bound to pledge that he would defend his guest as if they were his own family while they were there, to the death if necessary. This idea puts a totally uncomfortable spin on the next Saturday night supper club.

To be fair, however, we do not necessarily need to be on sword-wielding alert against gangs of marauding oppressors in order to offer hospitality. Hospitality wears various faces, most of which are thankfully quite physically safe. Such hospitable love can be costly, nonetheless. If we are to love our neighbors as ourselves, a passing wave as we drive down the street is inadequate. We are, after all, not commanded to be merely friendly, but to love them. The cost may come in terms of being known, and in squelching the pride that might be wounded as a result of that genuine knowledge. Opening our homes to people opens ourselves to them. And unless you've got one of those houses with enough space that the guests don't have to see where you really live, they see part of you when they come into your home. The vulnerability can be a bit disconcerting (especially if your "powder room" also serves as a family bathroom, because there will come a time when you forget to clean it, and your guests will end up there, and they will know then, beyond a shadow of a doubt, that if indeed cleanliness were really next to godliness, you're on the outs—not that I'm speaking from experience).

Thank goodness, thank God, we need neither a finely appointed space nor a culinary degree to practice hospitality. In our home, we have neither, yet I think that, unawares, we may have entertained angels once or twice in this place. If not angels, we have at least shared some sweet fellowship.

A frequent occurrence in our home is a gathering of our immediate physical community: our neighbors, who are one of the things I love most about life on our street. These folks whose homes we look at every day have become accidental family to us. Had we not shared geography, I'm not sure these bonds of friendship would have been forged; we encompass a wide range of interests, world views, and life stages. Yet we all genuinely love each other and thus the hospitality flows among us in various forms, not always effortlessly but always joyfully. Meals passed among us have, if only momentarily, eased the bitter mourning of losing a parent or nursed the pains of a medical procedure. Several impromptu front porch meals have brought blessed relief from the "my fridge is empty and I don't have the energy to go to the store" syndrome. Friday evening happy hours have morphed into Friday night pizza parties accompanied by lively conversation that eases us out of a workweek. Some have even turned into sing-a-longs to music that strikes a common cord through the generations.

Not all gatherings are impromptu porch soirees, however. Many are intentional, labor-intensive occasions. Unless you have a huge freezer, remarkable organizational skills, and an impeccable culinary imagination, hospitality does not just happen. There is planning, there is shopping, there is preparing. It requires work. I believe the key to crossing the line from entertaining to practicing hospitality is when the work becomes overshadowed by the joy of serving and the pure enjoyment of the fellowship that results from the work.

Mabel encouraged me to practice hospitality. I learned some things from her about cooking, of course, but mostly she lived out the Scriptural command to "be eager to practice hospitality" (Romans 12:13 NLT) in front of me, a gentle living reminder that for those of us who call ourselves Christians, hospitality is indeed a command, not an option.

Even more than modeling what I ought to do and inspiring me to do it, however, she demonstrated the abundant blessing that is the result. The older I get, the more realize just how much our lives revolve around food on a day-to-day basis: all kinds of food in all kinds of places on all kinds of occasions. It's woven who we are as people. The every-day rhythms, the milestone markers, the mountaintop highs and the valley lows: most of these involve some kind of gathering around a table.

Life so often occurs around the breaking of bread: the scooping of a dinner casserole in the kitchen after the unremarkable routine of a weekday, the carving of a bird to celebrate a festive holiday, the icing of a cake to celebrate another birthday, or the gathering for a luncheon in the church to mark the painfully joyous home-going of a dear friend. These are the moments that make up life. When we're around the table, we fill our whole selves: the parts that rejoice or grieve, the parts that are new or old. We fill our hearts with the companionship that gives meaning to the rhythm and effort of our daily tasks; we fill our bodies with what we need to persevere in those tasks. We become whole.

It's no mistake that feeding people is what happens in both the peaks and valleys of our lives. Feasting, in some form, accompanies almost all the momentous occasions of life. When friends grieve the loss of a loved one, our impulse is often to feed them: sustain them in body while their spirit is famished and keep the body going until the spirit is revived. When babies are born, we like to fill freezers full of meals to eliminate one small burden from the shoulders of the new mama. Weddings are typically celebrated with some type of feast; remember, Jesus himself chose a wedding feast as the venue for his first public miracle.

All of this is hospitality. It doesn't necessarily require much in terms of what we actually put out on the plates, but it does require our whole heart.

"The thing of it is," Mabel would say, "I'm just happier when I'm making other people happy."

Recipes: Main Dishes

Although Mabel never wanted to serve just an ordinary meal, her midwestern roots nonetheless meant that deep down she always had a bit of a "meat-and-potatoes" approach to her cooking.

Beef Brisket

Mabel was from Iowa, where good, rib-sticking meat was an expectation. This recipe produces a tender, flavorful crowd-pleasing roast. She usually planned for between 1/4 - 1/3 lb. of meat per person, as long as several accompaniments would be served.

5 -7 lb. beef brisket
2 envelopes onion soup mix
1 bottle Baby Ray's (or your favorite) barbecue sauce

Refrigerate brisket overnight. For the best flavor, rub with onion soup mix before refrigerating for flavors to absorb. (If you miss this step, you can still rub the meat with the soup mix right before placing in the oven.) Take the brisket out of the fridge an hour before cooking and let it go to room temperature. Place the brisket in a large roasting pan. Rub with onion soup mix if you not have already done so, then cover with barbecue sauce. Place in a rack in a roasting pan with the fat side up (so the juices drip into the meat), and cover tightly with foil. Roast for at least 3 hours at 325°, until the internal temperature of the meat reaches 175°.

Turn off the oven, and let the brisket sit, covered, for another hour. When cool enough to handle, remove the brisket and cut into slices against the grain. If necessary, strain fat out of the roasting pan (pour through a fine mesh strainer) and return juices to pan. To thicken the gravy, mix one Tbsp. corn starch with hot water, and add to the pan juices. Whisk continually until gravy thickens.

Put the sliced beef back in the roasting pan with the gravy and re-heat on low heat.

Serves 10-12

Beef Roast

5-6 lb. beef (boneless eye of round)   3 c. soy sauce
2 tbsp. olive oil   1 c. Worcestershire sauce

Seasoning Rub

2 stalks celery
1 tsp. onion powder
1 tsp. garlic powder
1 tsp. coarse salt
1 tsp. paprika
1 tsp. dried crushed rosemary
1 tsp. dried thyme

Preheat oven to 500. Take the roast out of the fridge and let it sit on the counter to bring to room temperature – about 45 minutes. Rub roast all over with olive oil, then lightly prick the meat all around with a fork. Rub seasoning rub mixture thoroughly onto all sides of the meat. Place on a rack in a roasting pan with the fat side up. Pour soy sauce and Worcestershire sauce over the meat. Cut celery into a couple pieces and place on top of the roast.

Roast uncovered for 15 minutes until browned. Reduce oven temperature to 300 and continue to roast until meat thermometer registers 140 degrees, usually about 20 minutes per pound.

Remove roast to a cutting board and tent with foil. Let sit for 15 minutes. Meanwhile, mix 2 tbsp. corn starch into ¼ c. cold water and whisk thoroughly. Pour corn starch mixture into roast drippings. Stir constantly over medium heat until mixture boils gently and thickens into gravy. To darken, add a small amount of darkening sauce such as Kitchen Bouquet. Season with salt and pepper if needed.

Slice meat against the grain. Pour gravy over sliced meat and serve.

Serves 10 - 12

Mabel's Famous Hot Chicken Salad

Often, there were just too many folks at Mabel's events for beef to be a financially feasible main dish. In that case, her famed hot chicken salad was the star of the buffet line for a large crowd. This recipe has been served at weddings, bridal showers, camp brunches, and church lunches. It works almost anywhere and anytime.

3 c. toasted bread cubes or croutons	1 tsp. salt
8 c. diced or shredded cooked chicken	½ tsp. pepper
4 ½ c. grated sharp cheddar cheese	2 ½ c. mayonnaise
1 c. slivered almonds	5 oz. bag potato chips OR
½ c. chopped onion	1 c. grated cheese mixed w/ 3 c.
6 tsp. lemon juice (fresh is best)	croutons (optional)

In a large aluminum foil pan, combine all ingredients except the last one; mix well. Spread evenly in the pan; top with chips or cheese/crouton mixture.

Bake at 350° for about 25 minutes.
Serves 25

<u>Tips:</u>

- ❖ Mabel's easy way to prepare cooked chicken: Season boneless chicken breasts with salt and pepper. Place in a 9x13 baking dish and add water or chicken broth to generously cover the bottom of the pan. Cover with foil and bake at 300 for about 40 minutes. Turn off the oven and leave the pan and chicken in the oven covered, for an hour. Let it cool, then shred with a fork. This can be prepared ahead of time and frozen in zip lock bags as well.
- ❖ The above recipe is the one Mabel gave out, rolled on pretty parchment paper and tied with colorful ribbon, as favors for her 100th birthday soiree. When working with her and preparing this dish, however, (and when she wasn't looking!) we reduced the amount of mayonnaise by at least ½ c. and generally found that most folks barely noticed the missing mayo (and some even preferred it).

Cold Chicken Salad

This recipe is a close runner-up to Mabel's hot chicken salad. It is another budget friendly dish for large crowds and can be served in a variety of presentations. Some ideas are listed below.

8 c. diced or shredded cooked chicken	1 tsp. salt
1 c. coarsely chopped walnuts or slivered almonds	½ tsp. pepper
	2 ½ c. mayonnaise (see note above)
6 c. diced celery	1 tsp. Dijon mustard (optional)
1 c. diced purple onion	
6 tbsp. lemon juice (fresh is best)	
4 c. halved red or green grapes or 2 c. chopped pineapple	

- Add a few tablespoons of chopped, fresh dill for an interesting flavor.

Mix all ingredients together in a large bowl. Chill in the refrigerator for an hour.

Serves 25

Serving suggestions:

- ❖ In a buffet, serve in one large bowl. Arrange small bunches of grapes around the edges of the bowl, and place sprigs of fresh dill in the center as a garnish.
- ❖ For individual servings, arrange a bed of greens on a luncheon plate. Top with chicken salad garnished with fresh dill. Sever alongside tomato wedges
- ❖ Scoop chicken salad onto bottom half of a croissant. Top withsliced avocado and the top half of the croissant.
- ❖ For a really special presentation, fill hollowed out tomatoes with chicken salad. Serve on a large lettuce leave. (See Bridal Shower Brunch on p. ????)

Brunch Casserole

1 loaf of sliced bread (white is best, but wheat is fine)	2 c. shredded cheddar cheese
	4 c. milk
2 lbs. of browned sausage, OR leftover spiral sliced ham, diced	2 tsp. each of salt, dry mustard, and garlic
12 eggs, beaten well	

Butter slices of bread (white is usually the favorite) and break into pieces. Place buttered side up in an aluminum tray sprayed with non-stick cooking spray. The bottom of the tray should be covered.

Cover bread with your choice of meat and cover meat with grated cheese. In a large bowl, whisk together eggs, milk, ground mustard, garlic powder and salt. Pour over all. Refrigerate overnight. Cook, covered with foil, 45

minutes at 350° until bubbly. Remove foil for the final 10 minutes. Let sit for at least 5 or 10 minutes before serving.

Serves 15

❖ Halve the amounts listed above and make in a 9x13 pan for an excellent make ahead casserole for holidays, or for a take along to a brunch. It's also delicious heated up the next day.

Tortellini Salad

1 1 ½ lb. package of sweet peppers, diced	1 lb. of grape tomatoes
1 large seedless cucumber, peeled and diced	1 5 lb. pkg. cheese tortellini
2 6 oz. cans of olives	1 33 oz. contained Vidalia onion vinaigrette (or other preferred dressing)

Prepare tortellini according to directions. Toss with vinaigrette and let sit for a couple hours. Toss with the remaining ingredients.

This salad can be a main dish at a luncheon and can be adjusted to fit almost any palette. It's delicious with almost any combination of vegetables. I tried it once with broccoli florets and dried cranberries. If budget is a concern, this is a relatively low budget dish that fills people up.

Serves 25

Roasted Salmon

2 3 lb. salmon filets	½ stick of butter for EACH filet
4 tbsp. chopped fresh dill for EACH filet	salt and pepper to taste

Salt filets. (If the filet has a portion that is a lot thinner than the rest of the piece, you may want to cut that off as it will roast more quickly than the

rest of the filet). Let sit for about 10 minutes. Melt the butter and chopped dill. Pour some onto a foil lined baking sheet. Place the filet on the foil. Pour the rest of the butter mixture over the filet. Bake at 475⁰ for twenty minutes. Fish will flake easily with a fort when done. Slice carefully and lift slices from skin with a spatula. Serve with extra dill butter, if desired, and fresh lemon wedges.

Serves 12

Roasted Salmon with Dill Sauce
(just a little fancier than recipe above)

2 3 lb. salmon filets	Dill Sauce:
2 tsp. lemon pepper seasoning	1/3 c. sour cream
1 small onion, sliced into rings	1/3 c. mayonnaise
6 lemon slices	1 tbsp. finely chopped onion
¼ c. butter	1 tsp. lemon juice
	¾ tsp. dill weed
	¼ tsp. garlic salt
	Pepper to taste

Whisk together all ingredients for sauce. Set aside.

Place salmon skin side down on a foil lined, lightly greased baking pan. Sprinkle with lemon pepper and onion salt. Top with onion and lemon. Dot with butter. Fold foil around salmon; seal tightly. Bake at 350° for 20 minutes. Open foil carefully to let steam escape. Broil for 8 minutes until fish flakes easily. Cover with sauce and serve.

Serves 12

❖ Because salmon is often pricey, Mabel did not serve this dish often to large crowds. However, it was often a favorite at smaller gatherings such as Women's Club meetings and bridal showers.

Crab Cakes

1 lb. crabmeat (lump crabmeat is best)	½ tsp. salt
1 c. Italian seasoned bread crumbs	¼ tsp. pepper
1 large egg	1 tsp. Worcestershire sauce
¼ c. mayonnaise	1 tsp. dry mustard
1 tsp. baking powder (to keep the crab cakes fluffy)	

For Maryland crabcakes, add 2 tbsp. Old Bay Seasoning to seasoning mix.

Spread crab meat on a paper towel. Pick through to make sure no bones remain. In a mixing bowl, mix bread crumbs, egg, mayonnaise and seasonings. Add crab meat and mix GENTLY but thoroughly. Gently form into patties (8 – luncheon size patties; 4 – dinner size patties). Place on a wax paper lined plate and chill in the fridge for at least ½ hour to help the crab cakes stay together better. Fry in hot oil until lightly browned, about 3-4 minutes on each side. Fry in batches so that you do not crowd the pan.

Serve on a lettuce leaf with a side of bottled tartar sauce or remoulade sauce.

Serves 4

Barbecued Shrimp

3 slices bacon, cooked and crumbled	1 tsp. black pepper
1 stick butter	½ tsp. oregano
2 tbsp. Dijon mustard	2 cloves garlic, crushed
1 ½ tsp. chili powder	2 tbsp. Old Bay seasoning
¼ tsp. basil	½ tsp. Tabasco© or other hot sauce
¼ tsp. thyme	1 ½ lb. medium shrimp, thawed and deveined

In a saucepan, combine crumbled bacon, butter and all seasonings. Simmer for five minutes, until well combined. Arrange shrimp in one layer in a baking dish. Pour sauce over top, making sure that all shrimp are coated well. Bake 30 minutes at 375, stirring once during baking. Serve hot.

Serves 6

Tea Sandwiches

Assorted tea sandwiches are perfect for any type of afternoon gathering: bridal or baby showers, book club meetings, or tea with friends. Make enough so that you have a minimum of 4 sandwiches per person. When cutting, always use a serrated knife and cut gently so you do not crush the bread. How many tea-size sandwiches you are able to cut from each large sandwich will depend on the shape you cut. Serving a variety of shapes is interesting if the lack of uniformity doesn't bother you. Mabel loved to serve several varieties in different shapes. Following are some of her favorites.

White bread with cucumber

Spread softened cream cheese on white bread. Top with thin slices of peeled cucumber. (Seedless English cucumbers are usually best.) Top with chopped fresh dill and another slice of white bread. Gently cut rounds with a round cookie cutter.

Note: With a 2 ½ in. round cookie cutter, you can usually get two sandwiches from each slice of bread. There will be some waste. If this bothers you, slice the bread first and then assemble the sandwiches. There will be less waste, but a bit more work. Using a smaller round cutter, you can usually get three sandwiches if you use a 2 in. cookie cutter.

Variations: add smoked salmon (after slicing into rounds); use chopped mint instead of dill

Wheat bread and pimento cheese

Spread wheat bread with pimento cheese. Top with another slice. Cut off the crusts and then cut diagonally into 4 triangles.

Raisin bread and strawberry cream cheese

Spread raisin bread generously with strawberry cream cheese. Top with another slice. Cut the crust off the bread. Then, cut diagonally into 4 triangles.

Egg salad

With a fork, mash 4 peeled, hard boiled eggs. Mix in about 2 tbsp. mayo, 2 tbsp. mustard (whatever kind you prefer), and salt and pepper to taste. Spread onto bread and top with another slice. With a serrated knife, gently cut off crusts, then cut sandwiches lengthwise into 4 rectangles.

> Variations: Add ½ tsp. curry powder for curried egg salad; add 4 tbsp. finely chopped ham chunks for ham/egg salad; add 2 tbsp. chopped green olives; add 2 tbsp. finely chopped cooked bacon and 1 tsp. horseradish

Crab salad

Mix together 2 hard-boiled eggs chopped, 4 cups of canned crabmeat, 1 cup of mayonnaise, the juice of one fresh lime, a tbsp. of paprika, and salt and pepper to taste. Spread on twelve-grain bread and top with another slice. Cut off the crusts, and slice lengthwise 3 times to get four rectangles.

❖ To keep your sandwiches from drying out, place them in a plastic container once assembled. Cover with wax paper, and place a very slightly damp paper towel over the wax paper. Store in the fridge, and arrange on a platter immediately before serving.
❖ For an attractive presentation, serve sandwiches on tiered platters.

Part Four
Sweet Finale

Let me grow lovely growing old, so many fine things to do.
Laces, ivory, gold and silks need not be new.
~Karle Wilson Baker

Lord of the Vine

"In wine there is truth."
~Pliny the Elder

Mabel was by no means a wine lover. Sitting on our patio with a small group of friends one fall evening by our firepit, as we poured a ruby red cabernet sauvignon into our own glasses, she quipped that she "would not participate in our sin with us." But she often served wine at her events; she recognized the part it can play in making an occasion lovely. As a farmer's daughter, she believed that what comes from the earth is good and meant to be enjoyed. We tried, once or twice, to share with Mabel our enthusiasm for the fruit of the vine, and for the beauty and artistry that can come from a bottle of wine, as well as the sweet communion that flows among the folks who share it. She told us she would stick with food and save the wine for us. Although our love of beautiful wine does not necessarily provide us opportunities to serve others be feeding their bellies, as Mabel did, it does provide occasions to feed souls as we enjoy God's lavish abundance.

Several times a year, we, along with our dear friends Pam and Mark, leave the bounds of the Beltway for the bucolic vineyards of the Virginia countryside. As we leave behind the six-lane superhighway and pass into the cooling shadow of Virginia's Blue Ridge, we recalibrate. Here, where the drone of traffic fades away, we pause to savor the beauty of creation and the artistry of the wines produced there amidst the backdrop of vine-laced hills. It's a soul-refreshing retreat for us, a day's respite from the customary clutter and noise of the everyday and a delightfully concrete reminder to us of the bounty of God's good and plentiful gifts.

I'm sometimes tempted to believe that life out here in these hills might be somehow spiritually superior to the lives that most of us conduct in the suburbs and cities. But that is not the case. God created us to be in community, no matter where we are, and it is from that community that we can derive loveliness. The great 4th century theologian St. Augustine envisioned the Christian community (both now and in the age to come) as a *City of God*. We go to cities to celebrate the enduring beauty of works of art in our great museums, to witness the imaginative genius of great architects displayed in the buildings we walk past, and to observe sporting events in our stadiums that give credit to the amazing capacity of the human form. All these endeavors, just like that of making a beautiful wine, ultimately bring glory to God.

Still, a different kind of pause possesses our souls at this place. The afternoons we spend here are lively, fun times, just like anyone would expect from an afternoon of wine tasting at a vineyard. But they're not the rowdy, bachelorette party kind of fun that sometimes happens at wineries. This winery is unusual in its understated atmosphere. Large groups are discouraged; folks come here to learn about and appreciate the craft and artistry shared by this vintner. The winemaker, Jim Law, has spent decades getting to know his terroir—his land—and how to coax out of it the choicest grapes to ferment into wine. They create art here in the way that the medieval author Dante defines art: creating a thing of usefulness and beauty out of the natural resources provided by God.

Most of the time, the four of us will go down into the cellar for a special tasting. It's cool and dim and muffled down there, among the barrels topped by flickering candles. Once, either because he sensed our anticipation or because he pegged us as eager to learn more about his craft, our cellar host led us down a narrow, oak-perfumed aisle between the barrels, where he unstopped a barrel and tapped the wine directly into our glasses.

"This wine is good now," he said. And we agreed. "But give it some time and it will be impeccable." Later, he gave us a taste of a similar wine, bottled and aged, to show us how beautifully complex and nuanced the wine could become. "This," he said, "is the art of winemaking."

I love coming here with our friends because Mark, especially, is so intuitively knowledgeable about wine. He's a smart guy— a rocket scientist in his day job—and he enlivens our conversations with his knowledge of things like the process of fermentation and the different varietals in Bordeaux blends.

In the cellar, we gather around a long wooden table to learn something of the special wines reserved for those who come down here. In the subterranean hush punctuated by merry laughter, we're invited into a deeper attentiveness as we listen to the winemaker talk about the grapes that have evolved into what is now in our glass.

He speaks of his wines almost as a parent might discuss his children—how this one suffered because of an unexpected late frost and needed tender care to be coaxed to ripeness; how this young vine produced fruit vigorously, almost recklessly, and needed disciplined pruning; how this unfortunate one was plagued by an onslaught of nefarious pests; or how circumstances created near perfection at harvest for this vine.

Clearly, winemakers have an intimate connection with the land and therefore a keener sense of the interconnectedness of all facets of creation: human, animal, plant, and mineral. This knowledge affords them a heightened appreciation for the beauty that results when creation treated as a precious gift to be used gratefully and thoughtfully. This is the heart of the Cultural Mandate in Scripture; this is what it means to have dominion over the earth.

Appreciating wine, especially the type produced by vintners whose craft is governed more by their artistry than by market forces, demands of us a certain attentiveness. Down in the cellar, the sounds of life are muted while we few gather around the table to listen, to learn, to savor, to laugh. Whether comparing blends or varietals, our guide first sets for us a stage: the conditions at harvest, the peculiarities of each grape, the container it went into, the nuances of its evolution as it lay in the wine racks. Before our first sip, all our senses have been prepared: the descent into the dimness of the cool cement and oak hush, the aromas of fruit or spice or mineral, candles flickering on rows of oak barrels.

The guide stops then, to listen to our reactions as we listen to each other. We delight together, though the experience is unique to each of us. And we become more acquainted with our friends, their preferences, their sensibilities. Some of our delight is rooted in gratitude that folks have worked, sometimes for over 30 years, cultivating the best grapes, learning when to harvest them, perfecting the blending, bottling, and storing process, mostly for the sake of the beauty that emerges in the shared sips of sensual delight.

Though we are captivated by the discoveries in the glasses set before us, there is much more than the appeal, as pleasant and as good as it might be, to our five senses that converges here. In the wine cellar, here with dear friends who share our faith, we've stepped into a heritage that is imbued with the most awesome of truths: this fruit of the vine that gladdens our hearts is also a symbol of the blood that was shed by the Lord of this creation and that will ultimately redeem all of creation, human and non-human, to perfect harmony.

Christians especially have the freedom to acknowledge that we've been set down by God in a physical world full of very good things created by a perfect and awesome Creator. We're not merely waiting for a better world in Heaven, because some of Heaven is here now, a gracious hint of the perfected future Earth. We're meant to care for it, use it, benefit from it, and enjoy it. Farmers get this; gardeners get this; vintners get this.

Jesus began his public ministry with wine: he turned the water into wine at the wedding in Cana. And this was no watered-down version of Boone's Farm Strawberry Wine; this was beautiful, choice wine, without which the wedding festivities would have faltered. Not only did Jesus keep the young bridegroom from the embarrassment of the social faux pas of running out of wine during what was likely his first community event as an adult, but He also ensured the right conditions for a joyful celebration. It is right and good that the solemnity of the occasion be accompanied by merriment as well.

But this first miracle points a far more significant reality: the redemption that is offered by Christ, the culmination of which will be a feast beyond human comprehension. The Bible doesn't tell us that we will have a feast in heaven; rather, it says the kingdom of Heaven is itself a feast, a continual, luxuriant, sensory experience. What Jesus did at that wedding in Cana was a mere foretaste.

And we can't ignore the viticulture metaphors; in the New Testament, Christ is depicted as the vine and his people as the branches. In the Old Testament, blessing often comes in the form of a fruitful vineyard. Lush vineyards and fields that will yield an abundance of grain and oil await the Israelites in the Promised Land, where they are offered productive lives in communities marked by peace and joyful singing and dancing.

Hopefully, most of us have experienced the warm contentment that follows sharing a fine meal and a special bottle of wine with friends or family. Maybe, around the table, we have been blessed with engaging conversations or eased tension in relationships. The "wine that gladdens human hearts" (Psalm 104:15 NIV) sometimes evens gladdens enough to begin to repair some of our cracks in the our lives. Our unspoken yearning for all of creation to be set in right order again is addressed in these occasions. Our delight is magnified because we are sharing. We are pulled closer to the products of the earth, even as we are bound closer to whomever we are sharing it with. Though the connection may be brief—the merriment of strangers toasting in unison because they both know the bride or groom, the shared laughter around a banquet table, the kinship found in appreciating a particularly well-crafted vintage—all threads of creation, human, animal, and vegetable, are woven more tightly. When the enjoyment grows from a shared gratitude to gratitude for the gracious Creator and author of all such goodness, the communion grows sweeter still.

I have no doubt that if we had ever been able to convince Mabel to come with us out to the winery, she would have been a fan of the peace and loveliness of it all. Even though she was certainly no wine connoisseur, the work that she did was similar to the work of the vintner. Both point us to the good gifts of creation that God gave us and to the privilege we have to exercise our creative impulse to make something lovely and pleasing. This impulse is inherent in us as image bearers of a creative God, but also rises out of a nurturing instinct. In the act of creating we both attend to our own soul and refresh the soul of others. Enjoying fine wine or a satisfying meal breaks apart the false body/spirit duality—the idea that our physical selves and our spiritual selves are two separate entities—that continues to plague much of modern theology. A close connection with creation, whether it be a farm, a vineyard, or a garden, cultivates an awareness of the coherent nature of all of life and helps us take joy in its goodness. We should all eat, drink, and be merry, for it is all the gift of a gracious Creator.

"The thing of it is," Mabel would say, "God gave us good things. Why shouldn't we enjoy them?"

Mabel Remembers:
The Last Woodside Hurrah

All of life for Mabel was a grand adventure. In whatever form it took, adventure was a calling for her. Bookshelves are stocked these days with instructions about how to find our true calling, how to figure out God's plan for our lives. It wasn't that complicated for Mabel. "The Bible tells me to lead the life God assigned to me (1 Corinthians 7:17), so that's what I do."

He gave her different assignments over the years. "I just wanted to keep having fun after college," she told me one day as we sat on our front porch swing. She loved to swing, but since her feet didn't touch the ground, I had to push us off from the floor to keep the swing going gently.

"So, teaching it was. There weren't a whole lot of options for us ladies in 1932 anyways." I wasn't sure whether a lesson or an exhortation was to follow. "It was a hard job back then, too," she told me, once again encouraging me in the midst of a teaching season in my life that had me stretched so tightly to the edges that one slight prick could make me pop. "But oh, how I loved it!" An exhortation in the form of a story, I thought. "You know, I only got to teach for seven years, but I still keep in touch with some of my students."

● ● ●

On June 21, 2008, 175 graduates of Woodside High School gathered in Des Moines for what we suspected might be our final meal together. For decades, we had been gathering, my students and me, every fourth year. They came from every corner of the United States. We chatted, we recalled many shared events, we broke bread together, we cried, we laughed, and then, we exchanged farewells. As I talked with these former students of mine, pictures of them as teenagers flooded my mind as if it was still the 1930's and not 2008. Though outwardly we all had changed a bit, we were still had the same hearts that we had back in that school in the late 1930's.

When one of the students told his wife he was going to the reunion just to see Miss Sawhill, she responded, "If you are well enough to get around the block with your walker, you're well enough to go and I'll buy you the plane tickets." Those tickets were purchased, and we had a lovely visit.

Many of the students shared stories of their children and grandchildren; one proud grandfather announced with pride that his granddaughter had become a Rhodes Scholar and was about to enter Harvard Medical School. Her husband, a West Point graduate, would join her at Harvard. So many of us and our families had gone on to serve the Lord well.

We bid each other tearful farewells, knowing we would probably not see each other again this side of Glory. "We will meet again," I assured them all, "around that Great Throne. What a wonderful day we have to look forward to!"

Death Where is Thy Sting?

"For I am convinced, that neither life nor death, neither
angels nor demons, neither the present nor the future,
nor any powers, neither height nor depth, nor anything
else in all creation, will be able to separate us from
the love of God that is in Jesus Christ our Lord."
~Romans 8:38-39

At 103, Mabel was no stranger to death. She had said good-bye to parents, siblings, countless friends and acquaintances, many a generation younger than her. No doubt that at her age, thoughts of death broke into her days on a regular basis, though her exuberance about life—both this one and the next—left not a single square inch for fear to take root. I have met few people who love life as ferociously as Mabel did, nor have I met many who held life as loosely. Perhaps that is why the Lord granted her a passing without struggle; she merely went to sleep one night and woke on the other side. I can only imagine the joy that greeted her at the "great throne" reunion that she had promised to her friends.

My husband Frank, though about 50 years shy of Mabel's century of experience, is one of those who might be almost as familiar with death as Mabel was; it was an unspoken understanding between the two of them. His familiarity grew out of his experiences in both his career and his personal life. Throughout his 30 or so years managing continuing care retirement communities, death has been a frequent visitor. Too often, he has had the excruciating privilege of holding a trembling hand or hearing a final breath before a soul passed through to the other side. He has witnessed many beautiful, age-ravaged friends leaving this world reluctantly, but peacefully; he has also seen a look of utter fear turn to desire in the brief moment that a person approaches the veil between life and death.

But death has touched him much more personally as well, when he lost his young wife to a heart condition and then lost his father, his best friend, just a couple of years later. Frank trudged the deep, solitary valley of grief while simultaneously trying to shoulder some of the grief of his two young kids. His life went on, and the fading shadows quietly embedded themselves in his heart—forever there, but eventually woven back into joy.

Some might despair of the heaviness, the injustice, the weariness of that bone-crushing grief, the kind of grief that testifies to us that death is a violence so unnatural that our minds tels us to avoid it at all costs. We were not meant to die. In the face of this kind of death-grief, I have seen Frank cling to grace, because this most heinous of all sufferings makes into reality the sweetest of all paradoxes: death is merely the entry into real life for those who believe. Mabel also knew this, and it inoculated her from fear and protected her joy.

I have a feeling that when I die, one of the things I will be most surprised at will be the thinness of that veil that separates life from death. We often get so wrapped up in our physical material realties, that we lose the ability to acknowledge the spiritual reality that is just as present.

In *The Great Divorce,* C.S. Lewis' brilliantly imaginative book about heaven and hell, he offers a picture of heaven as a supremely concrete reality that far exceeds anything our limited minds can comprehend on this side of eternity—and one that is so far superior that nobody would want to come back. This, Frank says, was the aspect of his wife's death most difficult for him to come to terms with. He knew that even if she could return, even with young children and a husband who still yearned for her, she would not choose to come back here. And yet, this knowledge is also one of the realities that most fuels his hope—hope in a future reunion— not, of course, as husband and wife; Scripture is clear that there is no such relationship in Heaven, but as something sweeter and purer than we can understand in this life on earth.

A book about food may seem a strange place to contemplate death. It is, however, these physical bodies that we feed every day that will one day be made into something new. And it is in feeding these bodies, both spiritually and physically, that Mabel found such joy over the years. She must have felt, at least in her post-100 years, a very palpable sense of standing at the edge of that veil. Yet her joy never diminished as she peeked through the curtain, nor did she succumb to despair, reluctant acceptance, or even desire to escape from the ravages of old age that might plague some of us.

I only once heard Mabel pine for her younger days. We sat in the rustic wood furniture outside theour little cabin home at at Camp Hemlock. Our kitchen crew was relaxing together after a full day of work. We had just finished reviewing our to-do list for the next meal when Mabel slipped into reflecting on her full life and the many annual trips she had made to this camp at different times. Each of us offered our insight as to which phase of our own lives we thought had been the best. "You know," she said looking off at Hemlock leaves twittering in the breeze, "I just wish I was 90 again."

Ever the Proverbs 31 woman, Mabel could laugh at the days to come, because she knew that Jesus has obliterated and we can look forward to the day when we will be perfect and complete, body and soul. "Someday," she told me, "this old body is going to be even better than it used to be when I was your age." We're reminded of this in the elements of bread and wine, food and drink, the holiness that seeps into the physical matter of our bodies. It all gets jumbled up into one. And so Mabel savored each day for what it was and had utter confidence in her future.

"The thing of it is," Mabel would say, "the best is yet to come."

Unburdened

"But those who hope in the LORD will
renew their strength. They will soar on
wings like eagles; they will run and not grow
weary, they will walk and not be faint."
~Isaiah 40:31

Mabel adopted this verse from the book of Isaiah as her life verse well before her centenarian status began to slow her down ever so slightly. Though her physical stamina was quite remarkable, the ravages of old age did not totally pass Mabel by. There came a time when, despite her Iowa-bred stoicism, she reluctantly admitted to some occasional weariness (though to be fair, it wasn't until she was past 100). But we could see that she did struggle, albeit valiantly and without complaint, as she grew older.

Although she never said it, giving up her car was perhaps the most unwelcome and unkind confrontation with physical decline she eventually faced. She abhorred the idea of giving up her independence, and she was stubbornly reticent to ask for help. So, despite her family's pleas that she consider giving up driving, she doggedly retained her place behind the wheel of her gold Buick long enough for us all to rehearse with her the potential dangers of continuing to drive when you can't really see all that well over the steering wheel. In true Mabel fashion, she would curtly remind us that God would protect her even on the Beltway, and, of course, He had things for her to do. Her minor traffic incidents, she insisted, were merely opportunities to share the Gospel. One such evangelistic opportunity presented itself after Mabel had turned 100.

The apartment building where Mabel had lived in Silver Spring, MD, since the 1970s sits right off an exit on the Capital Beltway. When my parents visited from Buffalo, NY, where traffic is exponentially calmer, they would grip their arm rests as we maneuvered across three lanes of traffic within couple of hundred yards to make it from the exit to the left turn lane into Mabel's neighborhood. But she did that nearly every day (with no gripping of anything!). On one day, however, not too long before her 101st birthday, she didn't make the lane changes as adeptly as usual, and obediently pulled that gold Buick over to the side of the road to talk with the officer whose lights were flashing in her rearview mirror.

The officer removed his sunglasses to make sure that he was seeing the numbers on her license correctly.

"1913?"

"Yes, I'm 100 years old, Officer."

She was close to home, and he just couldn't find it in himself to issue her a ticket.

"This ticket would be 100 dollars," he told her, "but I'm gonna let you go on home and get yourself some rest."

She was indignantly grateful. "Well, I'm not going to rest because I have 12 trays of sticky buns to make for our church luncheon this weekend, but I'll tell you what I'll do, Officer. I'm going to take that $100 dollars and put it in the offering plate on Sunday and then I'm going to pray for the safety of you and all your officer friends."

She did it all—the sticky buns, the $100 offering, and the praying. But she did not go home to rest. Mabel did not find her rest in the ceasing of activity, but in her reliance on Jesus for everything, even finishing her cooking tasks as she bustled about in her kitchen. She seemed impervious to the everyday weariness that too often plagues so many of us, prancing around in her leopard print shoes with the lightness of soul that freed her from much of the crushing load that drains most people as they age. Her ability to find that sweet soul-rest kept her actively working at her vital ministry serving people until the week before the Lord brought her home to Him when she was 103 years old.

I wondered often, sometimes aloud and in her presence (and with lots of company wondering along with me), how she could keep up that pace of cooking and talking and serving. My feet that have wandered the earth for about a ½ century less than Mabel's feet were achy and tired after a day with Mabel in that Camp Hemlock kitchen, preparing all the food for our church's youth group retreat. Mabel, on the other hand, would perch ever so lightly on one of the kitchen stools, gleefully anticipating how much the campers would enjoy the 11 p.m. snack, planning the next meal, and scanning the crowd of campers for the comedic stars of the upcoming skit night. The rest of us just wanted to go to bed.

Once, she told me the secret to her abundance of energy. "I could have never done all this if I had married," she said. "A man would have just slowed me down."

Unless, of course, his name was Frank McGovern. I often joked with her that if timing had been about five decades different, I might have had to keep a close eye on her; Frank was Mabel's later-in-life crush, we teased. How she admired him! Although Frank has a different brand of spunk than Mabel had (perhaps because he refuses to have anything to do with leopard print), he, too, is an unburdened soul, having learned as Mabel did the secret in Matthew 19:2 of "find[ing] rest for your souls."

Mabel continues to teach me even now as she moves unfettered among the souls in eternity. How I wish I could talk to her and tell her what I learn from her still. I'd tell her that she is the living example of the "rest" that is discussed in A.W. Tozer's *Pursuit of God* that we're discussing now in Sunday school class. I'd tell her we ladies talk about her frequently; we reminisce about the myriad ways we have been encouraged because we saw in her a way of being that we could grab hold of as well.

Tozer was a famous theologian and writer who was a contemporary of Mabel. He wrote in the mid-20th century; perhaps that time with its relative lack of distraction enabled him, as it did Mabel, the ability to better grasp some essentials of life. One chapter of Tozer's beloved classic, for example, speaks of the "blessed relief which comes when we accept ourselves for what we are and cease to pretend." Mabel lived that "blessed relief." She never pretended to be anything but Mabel for a moment in her life; she merely relished the life that God had given her and lived each day in grateful service, doing whatever it what He gave her to do that day.

In *The Pursuit of God,* Tozer talks of the personal burden that so many of us carry that prevent us from finding the coveted rest that often seemed to come so naturally to Mabel. Tozer identifies our problem as a heavy "labor of self-love" that wearies us. Admittedly, Mabel loved praise as much as the next person; she was human after all. Few things made her smile as brightly as compliments about her cooking. But rather than accepting praise as self-love, she pointed to God as the one who gave her the gifts to be able to do what she did; the burden of prideful self-love is one that she did not carry.

Tozer's next barrier to rest and peace is pretense: "the common human desire to…hide from the world our real inward poverty…a false sense of shame." The antidote offered to this element of the burden can be found in Matthew 18:3: "you…[must] become as little children." This verse, of course, has nothing to do with childishness, but has everything to do with childlikeness. The souls of little children are not burdened by pretense, and their unencumbered joy is infectious. The muck of life is somehow cleaned out of my heart when I see my grandbabies. Their delight in what is delightful, humorous, or surprising, is not sullied by envy or comparison. They enjoy for the sake of having something to enjoy. How hearts could be lightened if we regained something of our childlike-ness. Mabel had that quality; she glowed with pride over the lighthearted pranks she had participated in over the years, and her belly laugh at a good joke was infectious.

We are also burdened, Tozer says, by artificiality, a "desire to shine… [and] appear other than what we are." No doubt this is a common experience: we strive to be the clever one at the party to hide the depth of our fear of loneliness when we return home that night; we talk of our latest professional success to mask the insecurity that has been built despite decades of education and experience; and we craft our social media posts of our tastefully decorated homes inhabited by ideal families so we can hide the struggle and the pain and disappointment that is an inevitable part of life lived among sinful human beings trying to find their place in the world.

But none of these need burden us to the point of exhaustion, Tozer exhorts us, because we can have the "blessed relief which come when we accept ourselves for what we are and cease to pretend."

There were times for Mabel, just like for the rest of us, that the burdens of life weighed her down. But still, she exuded a rare peace that eludes many of us. I have often wondered if it came from her no-nonsense Iowa farm girl, Depression-era sensibilities, or if it came from an unquestioned and abiding devotion to the God that she met as an Iowa farm-girl. I think probably, all of those are mixed up together until one flows into the other so that trying to make a distinction is not useful. Whatever it was, I'm sure we'll have a lovely time discussing it when we meet again.

"The thing of it is," Mabel would say, "I just do what it is that God has for me to do that day, and then I go to sleep. Worrying about anything else is a waste of time."

The Best Day of My Life

"Today was the greatest day of my entire life!"

Mabel was walking uncharacteristically slowly down the carpeted hallway of a rehab facility, the random sparks of light reflecting off her gold sequined shoes incongruous with the walker she leaned on. Despite her unusually sluggish pace, though, her spirit was bright enough to lift even the most downcast of hearts. We meandered down the hallway, stopping to talk to everybody, most of whom had already come to know her during her short stay.

I waited expectantly. Had she finally met the man who wouldn't slow her down? Had she won the lottery? What could possibly be the source of her jubilance right now, as she was enduring this unpleasant trial in her life? I should have known better.

"I talked to so many people about Jesus!" she gleamed, guiding me into the beauty salon so I could see where they did her hair so nicely.

At the age of101, Mabel was recovering from her second fall in a as many months. In both cases, she had hit her head and required hospitalization. The culprit: exhaustion. Mabel had been keeping a catering schedule that would exhaust most people half her age.

Faint glimmers of spring were teasing us now, the shadows we saw through the windows getting a bit smaller every day. At the beginning of the holiday rush, Mabel had her first fall. It happened in the garage of her apartment building; she had a great spot, close to the elevators, and we were always grateful for the steps that parking spot saved her when she was emptying the remains of her catering events into the cart to take back to her apartment.

We had stood there together many times, unloading the unused butter, salad dressing, or leftovers from catering events into a cart that she took up to her 8th floor apartment. "Take this leftover brisket home," she offered. "You won't have to cook and Frank will have a nice dinner."

The non-perishable items—paper products, aluminum trays, unopened canned goods—would go back in the trunk for the next event. As she handed me items to be re-stocked in her trunk-turned-supply closet, she reviewed the success of the event and rehearsed what could be done better next time. Always, she sent me off with warm gratitude.

I wasn't with her when she fell, but I can picture the exact spot where she was standing, orange patent leather boots planted on the cold December concrete, surveying her trunk, wondering what she would need for her next event and what she could leave in her car.

She always had lists, but she didn't rely on them too much—she preferred the flexibility, and maybe even enjoyed the secrecy—of holding her plans loosely to herself. There was no going online to look at anybody else's ideas, and rarely a re-consulting of last year's list for the same event. For Mabel, every event was about who would be there this time, and what they would need. The only computer Mabel needed was her memory, and it was that memory into which she was reached as she looked into her trunk.

Although she would never admit that the five events she had catered that week had worn her down, her body revolted on her as her next to-do list swirled through her head, and she fell backwards onto the concrete. A neighbor who happened to be nearby and saw her crumple to the ground immediately called 911 and stayed with her until paramedics arrived. Much to her dismay, she did not go home that night but instead remained in the hospital, forced to cancel catering events for the near future.

Although not being able to provide her promised meals hurt her more than the smack of her head on the concrete, Mabel was not one to let any opportunity pass her by. Even as the black and blue spread under her eyes and her head throbbed, her primary focus rested on the folks who were in and out of her room, bringing her food, changing her bandage, taking her vital signs, reviewing her chart.

So she talked to them, all of them—doctor, nurse, volunteer. And they listened. They listened because they knew that this tiny giant of a woman who smiled at them and reached out with bent fingers to take their hand gently in hers had something to say that they want to hear. She had inhabited this earth for more than a century by that time, but that is not why they listened. They listened because living for so many years as a daughter of the King made Mabel a conduit of grace, even to those who don't know what grace is. A light shone through her wrinkled skin, wrinkles which she had neither the time nor the inclination to notice. She was too busy listening to them share their stories. And Mabel listened because she knew grace would work through her and cover each of her companions in exactly the way it needed to.

Six weeks and another fall later, she was back for some rest and more rehab, recuperating while having the time of her life. As she recuperated again, she listened to more stories and found more grace opportunities. Folks didn't need her chicken salad or her brisket here, but she sensed another need and got busy. One nurse slipped into her room at 2 a.m. to check on her, surprised but pleased to find Mabel awake. Mabel coaxed out of her a story of disappointment and pain. The two of them joined hands over the metal bar at the side of the bed to pray.

Later, a 90-year-old fellow rehab patient finally decided to get her hair done and finally take a walk through the hallways, just because Mabel did. And a physical therapist was congenially reprimanded for assigning exercises that are too easy for this 101-year-old. "You need to make me work harder," she told him, "so I can get home and get back to work."

"The thing of it is," Mabel said, "if you have Jesus, you always have something to give that people need. You just need to keep your eyes and ears open for the opportunity."

Thoroughly Modern Mabel

"People who say there are no useful activities for
old age don't know what they are talking about."
~ Cicero, *On Old Age*

A couple of days after Mabel passed away, Frank and I crouched in one of Mabel's walk-in closets with her great-niece Shanna, smiling at the colorful assortment of shoes, dresses, and bags shoved into every available inch of space.

Shanna pulled out the flouncy peach chiffon dress and recalled the stories Mabel told her about wearing it as a bridesmaid in the 1950s. Leopard print pumps and matching handbags lining the racks brought to mind images of Mabel click-clacking around a kitchen. Outfits of decades long past were jammed toward the back of the closet, while nearer to the front hung the clothing of more recent years. On one hanger was the memorable bright pink floral dress that about 700 of us recall when we remember her flitting around joyfully at her 100th birthday celebration. Next to it hung the slightly more casual, though certainly not more understated, orange dress and sweater set that she saved for brunch on the following October morning, a smaller gathering for Mabel's family and close friends.

Bright purses of all sizes and shapes hung on hooks. And of course, there were shoes. Rows of petite shoes in every color of the rainbow, dominated by leopard prints, stilettos, kitten heels, and the more recently worn flat shoes, which Mabel grudgingly consented to wearing only in her 90s.

Sagging closet rods spanned both sides of the closet, depicted a lifetime of weddings, church dinners, family celebrations, and even funerals.

Toward the back hung a particularly elegant creamy satin sheath, the kind of dress worn by a meticulously coiffed lady balancing a glass of sparkling beverage between manicured fingers as she charms an admiring audience. We pictured a young Mabel doing just that in decades past, as Shanna shared with us Mabel's recollections of wearing the dress to a wedding in 1940s. The fellas were all dressed to the nines, Mabel had told Shanna, but none so much that Mabel was interested in any of them. And besides, she was too busy with her work with the Navy to worry about much else. Shanna set the dress aside, with the hope that someday she might wear it in Mabel's honor, perhaps even at her own elegant garden wedding. Like Mabel, the dress is classic and timeless.

It was a strange way to mourn our friend, perhaps: camped out in her closet with her great niece, reminiscing about her outfits. But for those who know Mabel, it makes perfect sense. Mabel's iconic style, represented by these dresses and bags and shoes, gave us a tangible way to mourn her.

We wanted to be here in her apartment and among her things to have one last contact with the physical person of Mabel. She held all of her things loosely: her wardrobe was merely a way to express her personality, her Waterford and Royal Doulton were gifts waiting to be given to the right person at the right time, and her pretty china and serving ware were implements of her gracious hospitality to others. It was all part of who Mabel was.

There was to be no final viewing; Mabel's wish was to be cremated and buried among her family in Iowa. This, then, would be our last time with Mabel.

Her family had already begun the task of cleaning out her apartment, and although she was constantly gifting people items from the storehouse of goods she kept in the bathtub of her spare bathroom, under tables in the guestroom, and in the corners of her dining room, her home was still full of many of the items she used and loved. The dining room hutch was stacked with the platters and bowls, many of them familiar to me from the various bridal showers and the graduation parties she did for my family. She had begun to thin her collections by choosing items to give away for any number of occasions.

One particularly harried and busy year, Mabel, sensing my weariness, offered to help me with the annual Christmas party that Frank and I typically host for his Senior Leadership Team at work. She made several friends that evening, happily staying far past the time the food had been served and cleared away. I began to pack up her treasured Lenox punch bowl that we had used that evening, and she stopped me. "That's yours now," she said. "You need something pretty for your Christmas punch." How she loved to give!

All over her apartment were shoes: piles and piles of actual shoes to wear that matched every outfit in her closet (she had to have options, after all), colorful prints of shoes framed on the wall, dainty ceramic shoes for display, even a pie server shaped as a shoe. Mabel was never particularly concerned about trends—she would have preferred to set them rather than follow them, anyways—but she never minded being a little fuss over her latest Nordstrom purchase. Her wardrobe expressed the many facets of her personality: confident, unaffected, cheerful, and fun.

We sat in the closet, the three of us, reminiscing about when she wore this pink leopard print at the church banquet, or the last time we saw her wear those high heels at that church potluck in her late 90s. Being sensible about her wardrobe, however, was never a chief concern of Mabel's. On our annual Labor Day trip to Camp Hemlock in West Virginia, those of us who lovingly called ourselves "Mabel's kitchen slaves" always packed our typical camp kitchen wardrobe: old shorts, t-shirts and comfy sneakers. Not Mabel. Her camp preparations always included the purchase of some new camp duds. On one of our final camp trips with her, she kicked off the weekend serving breakfast in purple leopard print leggings, with a smart coordinated tunic and strappy sandals that made my feet ache just looking at them. She grinned from ear to ear, though, every time one of the high school girls came into the kitchen to admire her outfit.

Mabel's style was not about fashion or keeping up with the Joneses or anybody else. And it was certainly not about pretending to be an age that she wasn't. She was energetic, she was engaged, she was fun, but I don't recall anybody ever saying that Mabel was youthful. Her wardrobe escapades were not motivated by a desire to fool anyone about her age. She readily and proudly presented her age whenever and wherever it was appropriate. She announced it often, as a matter of fact: announcing her age was a badge of honor for Mabel. As I sat scrunched in the closet that evening among the 21st century Vera Wang dresses and the 1940s pillbox hats, it occurred to me that Mabel may have been one of the most modern women I have ever known. She wasn't modern because she kept up styles and trends, rather, she unaffectedly transcended them. Mabel was ageless; she was timeless.

Mabel's ideas of femininity wouldn't win her any popularity contests in mainstream culture these days. But her timeless way of living out her traditional, Biblical values could speak winsomely even to women who believe the false cultural narrative that things like serving people and working in the kitchen are demeaning women's work to be avoided purely for the sake of "girl power."

Her ideas were born of the place and time from which she came: a place where boys and girls were expected to work alongside adults on the farm, where church attendance, meals, and sometimes education were intergenerational affairs, and where terms like *adolescence* and *feminism* had not yet entered anyone's vocabulary. The world Mabel came from was one where boys were boys and girls were girls, and old age was respected without being dreaded because youth was not idolized.

Mabel didn't defy her age. In our youth-idolizing culture, to say a person defies her age is really code for "she doesn't look as old as she really is." What was so impressive about Mabel was that she refused to be defined by her age, but she also did not disregard her age. Although I only met her when she was in her late 80s, I knew her well enough to say with confidence that she didn't act like a teenager when she was in her 30s, nor, I am certain, did she act as if she was 100 when she was a mere 70.

And Mabel was most certainly no generational segregationist; she was equally at home among those her own age as she was with those born nearly a century later than she was. In the kitchen at Camp Hemlock, as we would take orders from her to prepare for the next meal—thaw the dough for sticky buns, slice the fruit for the salad—the teenage campers would drift in and out. We usually saw almost all the 50 or so of them in our kitchen at one point or another during the retreat.

They come, they would say, for ice, to fill their water bottle. To find out what the next meal is. To catch a break from the heat. A lot of the time, though, they came to see Mabel. Sometimes, their friends had told them about her leopard print leggings, and they came to evaluate and tell Mabel if the color worked well for her. Sometimes legends of her famous sticky buns, or her strawberry spinach salad, or her baked Alaska, or the kitten heels she click-clacks down the aisle at church drew them in. They popped into the steamy kitchen to see this 102-year-old style maven bustling in and out of the walk-in refrigerator and opening and closing the heavy iron doors of the camp ovens; they came to see her in action, but they stayed because she talked to them as she would talk to any of her friends.

Often, the conversation starts because Mabel had catered their parents or grandparents' wedding. Then, she would try to find out how they are doing at camp. For the ones who hung around the fringes of the crowd, the conversation would last a little longer. What school do they go to? What are they studying? Plans for college? Laced throughout the conversation would be the inevitable reflections on how God is working, has worked, will continue to work in their lives. Sometimes stealthily, sometimes bluntly, she pointed them to the reason they came to camp—to get to know their God better.

She always wanted to be in the know: Who won "Capture the Flag"? Were the veteran campers including the new kids? Who was going to steal the show on skit night? And she certainly did not mind the reminders that her camp food was not ordinary camp food. "No hot dogs and hamburgers here" could have been a Hemlock slogan. But in the end, it all boiled down to Jesus. No matter who she was talking to, no matter what their age or occupation or station in life, her preoccupation was always the timeless, ageless truth of the Gospel.

What made Mabel a modern wonder was her ability to step outside trends and time. She walked through her days with a boldness and lack of self-consciousness that enabled her to fit in with whomever and wherever she happened to find herself. She was truly a lady for all seasons.

"The thing of it is," Mabel would say, "God didn't put me on this Earth to fritter away my days getting old. I'll stay busy until the day He calls me home."

Recipes: Desserts

Excellent endings were important to Mabel. Because she was a fan of doing everything with as little fuss and as much efficency as possible, she saw no shame in relying on pre-made desserts from Costco. Their cakes and cookies are particularly well done. (My own daughters, both chocolate connoisseurs, served Costco chocolate layer cake at their weddings. The cost was so significantly lower than a traditional wedding cake that a comparison can hardly be made, and I didn't hear anything but compliments from the guests.) On occasion, however, Mabel would make her own sweet dessert. Here are her favorites.

Mabel's Famous Sticky Buns

Although sticky buns are not technically a dessert, they are sweet enough to be! This is Mabel's signature dish; she served sticky buns at some point in nearly every meal she prepared, whether as a sweet bread for brunch, an accompaniment at a luncheon, or a finale at a dinner. The recipe is simple, but it's not always easy to achieve the perfect sticky bun. In customary form, Mabel didn't follow any recipe, but would just throw in a little more sugar here, a little more butter there. After helping with hundreds of trays, and tracking the amounts that were used, I have found that the following recipe is the one that typically results in the best sticky buns. Remember, though, making Mabel's sticky buns is an art, not a science!

2 – 2 ½ c. brown sugar   ½ lb. butter
3 1 lb. loaves prepared frozen bread dough

Thaw dough by placing in a warm place free of drafts. Allow to rise about ½ inch above the sides of the container, about 3 hours. Don't overthaw; dough should still have some firmness to it for best results.

Combine sugar and butter on the stove. Cook over medium heat until butter is melted and incorporated. The consistency should be such that the mixture runs slowly off a spoon held over the pot.

On a well-floured surface, roll out the dough into a rectangle of about 24 in. by 5 in. Cut the dough rectangle in half to make the next step easier.

Spread a thin layer of sugar mixture onto the dough rectangle. Roll up jelly roll style and cut dough into about 12 1 in. slices so that you end up with pinwheel rounds. (If you prefer larger, doughier buns, cut the slices larger.) If the slices get a bit mushed into an oblong shape when you cut them, adjust the shape back into a circle to get the prettiest buns.

Arrange the pinwheel rounds in a 12x18 aluminum pan that has been sprayed generously with cooking spray. Pinwheels should lightly touch, but shouldn't be smushed together in the tray. If there is any sugar mixture left over, drizzle it over the buns. Cover with foil and allow them to sit for at least an hour to rise more. (At camp, the earliest riser would take the buns out of the fridge and start the coffee. They would typically rise for about 3 hours before we baked them.)

Bake, covered with foil, at 375° for about ½ hr. Remove the foil for about the last 5 minutes of baking. The top should be golden. Let sit for about 5 minutes (no longer because they'll stick to the pan), then invert onto a large tray or clean surface. Let sit for about 15 minutes, then pull pinwheels apart carefully with forks.

Makes about 6 dozen medium sized sticky buns.

Some options, should you choose to go beyond Mabel's basic recipe:

*Spread chopped pecans along the bottom of the pan before arranging the dough pinwheels.

*Add some peeled, chopped apple to the dough rectangle before rolling it.
*Add 2 ½ tbsp. cinnamon to the sugar mixture.

Hot Fudge Sundaes

2 cans Sweet Evaporated milk   4 squares semi-sweet baking chocolate
1 gallon vanilla ice cream

Combine milk and chocolate either in a double boiler or in a sauce pan over medium heat. If using a sauce pan, be sure to stir often to avoid sticking. As the sauce thickens, add hot water to thin to the consistency you desire. Spoon the sauce over scoops of vanilla ice cream.

Serves 16

Baked Alaska

For pie:
2 pre-made pie shells   1 gallon ice cream, any flavor

For meringue:
12 egg whites for meringue   1 tbsp. vanilla
1 c. sugar   ½ tsp. cream of tartar

Prepare the pie shells according to package directions. Allow ice cream to soften enough to fill and spread into pie shells. Cover with plastic wrap and chill in a freezer until ice cream is hard again.

To make meringue, whip the egg whites and cream of tartar with an electric mixer until foamy, about 3 or 4 minutes. Add vanilla and sugar and continue to whip until stiff peaks form. Spoon meringue over ice cream with a spatula. Brown the meringue with a kitchen blow torch, being careful not to get closer than about 6 inches from the pie. If you do not have a blowtorch, bake the pie in a 500 oven for about 4 minutes, until peaks are slightly browned. (We found this method to be a bit messy, as it was difficult to achieve nice browned peaks and keep the ice cream from melting.) Slice pie into 8 slices and serve immediately.

Serves 16

Sour Cream Coffee Bread

1 c. butter	2 c. flour
2 c. plus 4 tsp. sugar	1 tsp. baking powder
2 eggs	¼ tsp. salt
1 c. sour cream	1 c. chopped pecans
½ tsp. vanilla	1 tsp. cinnamon

Cream butter and gradually add 2 c. sugar, beating until light and fluffy. Beat in one egg at a time. Fold in cream and vanilla. Sift flour, baking powder, and salt together and fold into mixture. Combine 4 tsp. sugar, pecans, and cinnamon. Put 1/3 of batter in Bundt pan; sprinkle with half of nut mixture. Repeat. Put rest of batter on top. Bake at 350 for 1 hour.

Serves 8

Part Five
Mabel's Menus

One of the things about Mabel that amazed so many of us was that she served large groups of people far more easily than most of us can ever imagine doing. Mostly, she could do that because of her firm conviction that she was doing what the Lord had called her to do. But, in addition to that, she kept things simple and revisited favorite dishes often, she cultivated capable and willing kitchen help, and she did not expect perfection. And always, always, she approached every event with bold and utter confidence that the Lord would provide all she needed to feed everybody who needed to be fed. I never saw anyone walk away from one of Mabel's events hungry.

For those of us who want to answer the call to practice hospitality but lack the confidence to make that happen, Mabel's menus might be that boost of confidence that we need. Following are some sample menus of events that Mabel catered. She would remind all of us, of course, that no matter what is on the menu or how well it is prepared, the most important thing to remember is that the fellowship is more important than the food and bringing glory to God is the most important of all.

How these menus are arranged: The first page contains the menu that corresponds to an event that I helped Mabel with. Each menu, of course, may be appropriate for all different kinds of events.

On the page(s) following the menu, you can find cross references to the page number of the recipes, information regarding amounts and number of servings, as well as any instructions or tips I learned from her. Some menu items may not have a corresponding recipe page number, simply because there is no recipe, but there are some brief instructions. Mabel was always a fan of keeping things as simple as possible.

Easy Dinner on the Patio for 8

One of the first things Mabel ever helped me with was this menu for a simple and casual dinner with friends. It may likely have been her strategy to increase my kitchen confidence so that I might readily help her more in the kitchen. It did, and I did. It was a win-win situation.

Cheese and Cracker Tray
Hot Crab Dip
Roasted Red Potatoes
Vegetable Bean Salad
Crab Cakes
Hot Fudge Sundaes

Notes/Instructions

<u>Cheese and Cracker Tray</u>
- Arrange 1 tray (instructions and tips on p. 124)

<u>Hot Crab Dip</u>
- Make 1 recipe (recipe on p. 15)

<u>Roasted Red Potatoes</u>
- Make 1 recipe (recipe on p. 47)

❖ You will likely have leftovers if you make an entire recipe with 5 lbs. of potatoes. You can cut them up and fry them for breakfast hashbrowns the next day. They also re-heat nicely.

<u>Vegetable Bean Salad</u>
- Make 1 recipe (recipe on p. 48)

<u>Crab Cakes</u>
- Make 2 recipes (recipe on p. 83)

<u>Hot Fudge Sundaes</u>
- Make 1/2 the recipe (recipe on p. 114)

<u>Additional Tips:</u>

❖ With the exception of frying the crab cakes, almost everything on this menu can be prepped before your guests arrive. The vegetable bean salad can be prepared a day ahead and refrigerated. Several hours before guests arrive, assemble the cheese and cracker tray and the crab cakes and refrigerate. Prepare the potatoes and spread on a baking sheet covered with foil. They can sit out on a counter for a couple of hours. Ingredients for the hot fudge merely need to be put into a sauce pan and heated on the stove on low heat during dinner.

❖ Set the table ahead of time.

❖ For a summer dinner on the patio, light citronella candles or torches around the perimeter of your eating area to keep the bugs away.

❖ Inviting folks for dinner is a beautiful means of fellowship. The easier you make it on yourself, the more likely you will be to do it. Keep a stash of paper plates and plastic ware in your pantry. Amazon has some reasonable options. I keep a silverware caddy full of elegant looking silver plastic ware in the pantry so that I can easily pull it out when we have folks over.

❖ Designate a counter or sideboard as a drink station and invite guests to help themselves.

Baby Shower Brunch for 20

Although Mabel thrived under the challenge of large gatherings, she relished the opportunity to do smaller gatherings as well. Because she relied mostly on tried and true recipes and menus, the events were relatively low effort and she could focus on her favorite activity: building relationships.

1 Fruit Tray with Creamy Fruit Dip
2 Assorted Cheese and Cracker Trays
Smoked Salmon Spread
20 Chicken Salad Filled Tomatoes
1 Strawberry Spinach Salad
1 Large Tray of Sticky Buns
Bakery Cake/Cupcakes or Petit Fours

Notes/Instructions

Fruit Tray

Beautiful fruit trays are a simple way to add elegance (and food!) to any event. Some tips:

- ❖ Use fruit that is in season. It doesn't really matter what fruit you have on the platter, but it should taste good, and should have a variety of color
- Slice/dice all the fruit first and let it drain a bit, then arrange it.
- Use a platter with a lip so that it doesn't drip on the table. (IKEA always has excellent options for trays.)

Mabel's preferences (if in season)

1 pineapple, quartered, removed from skin, then sliced into thin (1/2 inch) triangles
1 small seedless watermelon, cut in ½, then each ½ into quarters. Remove flesh from rind, and slice into thin triangle slices
2 cantaloupes, sliced or scooped into balls
2 honeydew melons, sliced or scooped into balls
1 lb. strawberries, stem intact
1 lb. blueberries
1 lb. grapes, divided into small bunches

To arrange:

- Arrange the pineapple (or other seasonal fruit) in an X formation on the tray. If you want to get real fancy, save the pineapple skin and stem and put the pineapple back in them.
- Arrange watermelon slices along the short edges of the platter
- Fill in empty spaces with sliced/balled fruit
- Place strawberries around tray in any gaps (usually groups of odd numbers looks best)
- Arrange grape bunches in the center.
- Fill in any bare spots with blueberries.

Optional: serve with Creamy Fruit Dip (recipe on p. ???).

<u>Cheese and Crackers Tray</u>

- 3-4 ounces of cheese per person

To arrange:

- Slice cheese ahead of time. (Unsliced discourages guests and slows down serving from the buffet.)
- Use a light and a dark colored cheese, and at least two cracker varieties.
- Alternate rows of crackers with rows of cheese.
- Garnish with something colorful: a couple of clusters of grapes or strawberries.

<u>Smoked Salmon Spread</u> (recipe on p. 19)
<u>Chicken Salad Filled Tomatoes</u>

This recipe is best for late summer when tomatoes are in season.

- Make a recipe of cold chicken salad (recipe on p. 79).
- Cut a small slice off the bottom of the tomato so that it will sit without rolling.

- Slice about the top third off the top of the tomato, and carefully scoop out the seeds and flesh inside with a melon baller, grapefruit spoon or other small spoon. (Save to make tomato sauce for spaghetti or pizza.)
- Fill the hollowed tomato with chicken salad. Garnish with a small sprig of basil or parsley from the garden.

Serve individually on a large leaf of lettuce

- ❖ A variety of differently shaped serving trays makes a buffet table more interesting. If you use a rectangle platter for fruit, use two round trays for cheese and crackers.

Strawberry Spinach Salad
- Make one recipe (recipe on p. 44)

Sticky Buns
- Make one recipe (recipe on p. 112)

Cake/Cupcakes

- ❖ Costco has plenty of desserts for purchase, but why not ask a baking friend to bring cupcakes? Mabel loved to involve as many people as possible in her events. People feel useful and more connected to others when they contribute something. Individual deserts also provide an easy opportunity to add visual interest to your table. Mabel would stack her small (pink, of course) pedestal serving dish on top of the larger one and arrange petit fours or cupcakes on them. Adding a vertical dish to the table is always visually pleasing.

Annual Church Officer Dinner for 25

Mabel was often called upon to help with events that were held to demonstrate appreciation for the service that folks had contributed. Because of the tireless and often unnoticed work undertaken by church officers over the year, Mabel liked to prepare something that was a bit more elevated than her ordinary fare.

Spinach Dip
Hot Clam Dip
Beef Roast
Roasted Salmon with Dill Sauce
Roasted Zucchini
Roasted Red Potatoes
Baked Alaska

Notes/Instructions

Spinach Dip
- Make two recipes (recipe on p. 16)

Hot Clam Dip
- Make two recipes (recipe on p. 18)

Beef Roast
- Make one recipe (recipe on p. 77)

Roasted Salmon with Dill Sauce
- Make one recipe (recipe on p. 81)

Zucchini Spears
- Make two recipes (recipe on p. 46)

Roasted Red Potatoes
- Make one recipe (recipe on p. 47)

Baked Alaska
- Make three pies (recipe on p. 114)

A Busy Hostess' Bridal Shower for 30

Cold Shrimp with Cocktail Sauce
Assorted Tea Sandwiches
1 large tray of Sticky Buns
Crab Dip with Crackers
Tray of Assorted Cheeses with a basket of crackers or Charcuterie Board
Vegetable Tray and Dip in a Bread Bowl
2 round chocolate Costco Cakes
Raspberry Sorbet Punch

Notes/ Instructions

Shrimp

- 2 lbs. medium, tail-on, steamed (most stores will steam them for you)
- For a nice presentation, fill a pedestal dish with crushed ice, and arrange the shrimp by "hanging" them over the edge, and laying them down on the ice in the middle. An arrangement of several large martini-style glasses filled with crushed ice will work as well.
- Serve with cocktail sauce: mix roughly equal amounts of ketchup and horseradish (less horseradish for less heat). Serve in small dishes next to the shrimp.

Assorted Tea Sandwiches (recipes on p. 84-85)

- Choose 3-4 varieties of sandwiches. Be sure to serve different shapes.
- Plan for about 4 sandwiches per person.
- Use a tiered tray for presentation. Graduated sizes of flat, stacked cake pedestals work nicely as well.

- ❖ Make the sandwiches a couple of hours before the event. Place them on a sheet of waxed paper and cover loosely with a sheet of waxed paper. To prevent them from drying out, put a slightly damp layer of paper towels on top of the waxed paper. Do not use a damp kitchen towel as the top layer, as that will likely make your sandwiches soggy.

Fresh Crab Dip with Crackers (recipe on p. 14-85)

Cheese/Crackers tray (instructions on p. 124)

If a cheese and crackers tray leaves you feeling like you want to step things up a bit, try a charcuterie board. A charcuterie board is assembled on a large, food safe (usually wood) tray. It is made up of cheeses, cured meats (pepperoni, salami, prosciutto), olives, and sliced baguettes or crackers and seasoned olive oil in small bowls for dipping. Two smaller charcuterie boards for a gathering of 30 would be plenty. To see how to make one, google how to make a charcuterie board (sorry, Mabs!).

Costco Chocolate Cake

❖ Mabel didn't often expend her greatest effort on making desserts. Because such good ones can be purchased from big box stores, this is an excellent place in your menu to let somebody else do the work. Nobody will mind, and your guests will be happier because you will be less stressed and will be able to spend more time with them. Costco usually carries deliciously decadent round chocolate cakes. To lose the big box store look and make your cake look more special and festive, do the following:

  • Put the cake on a pedestal server, and top with fresh raspberries in the center. Sprinkle some raspberries around the base of the cake as well.
  • Put a small posy of fresh flowers in the middle.
  • Or, google "grocery store cake hacks" for all kinds of clever cake dressing

Raspberry Sorbet Punch

Prepare an ice ring ahead of time: Place sliced strawberries and sliced lemons or limes or oranges at the bottom of a bundt pan. Pour 16 oz. bottle of ginger ale over all and freeze overnight.

For the punch, spoon one pint of raspberry sorbet into a punch bowl. Slowly pour a two liter bottle of lemon lime soda over the sorbet. Gently soften the sorbet with a spoon until it is mixed in; add the ice ring to punch bowl.

❖ Mabel loved to serve punch in traditional punch bowls. For the bridal or baby showers we did together at my house, we would set the punch bowl on a small side board and surround the base of the bowl with greens from my yard or clipped from the side of the road: forsythia branches in the spring, evergreen branches and berries during the winter. Most folks now are more likely to have upright beverage dispensers. Though you may have to break an ice ring into pieces to fit, the same simple décor principle can dress your drink station up a bit.

Luncheon for 40

Mabel often provided food for Bible studies, Senior luncheons, teachers' groups, etc. This menu is one she served to a variety of those groups: men, women, young and old. Although beef brisket is almost always a favorite, it can be a budget buster sometimes, unless you can find some good specials. For a lower budget option, substitute chicken salad (hot or cold) for beef brisket. A Costco sheet cake is one of the least expensive ways to serve dessert to a crowd; another option is to get several cartons of large bakery cookies. A safe amount is 6 dozen for a crowd this size.

2 large bowls of Strawberry Spinach Salad
2 trays of Beef Brisket (or chicken salad)
1 tray of Roasted Red Potatoes
4 bowls of Peas w/sautéed mushrooms
1 tray of Sticky Buns
1 large bag of dinner rolls (40 count) with butter
Iced Tea and Coffee
Sour Cream Coffee Bread

Working Lunch for 50

Because she started her own career as a teacher in the 1930s, Mabel held a special place in her heart for educators. She traversed the Washington, D.C. region providing food for various types of gatherings of private and public-school educators. She often prided herself on knowing principals and headmasters of most schools in four different counties. She liked to keep her "teacher food" easy, fun, and quick, because "you have to have a sense of humor if you're a teacher, and you'll need to get back to work quickly."

Fruit Tray with Creamy Dip
Hot Crab Dip
Hot Chicken Salad
Barbecued Shrimp
Broccoli Apple Salad
Sticky Buns

Notes/Instructions

Fruit Tray with Creamy Dip – 2 trays (instructions and recipe on p. 123)
Hot Crab Dip – 2 recipes (recipe on p. 15)
Hot Chicken Salad – 2 large trays (recipe on p. 78)
Barbecued Shrimp – 3 recipes (recipe on p. 83)

- In this menu, the shrimp serves as more of a side dish than an entrée. To serve as an entrée, double the amount of shrimp served, and reduce the chicken salad to one tray.

Broccoli Apple Salad – 3 recipes (recipe on p. 48)
Sticky buns – 3 trays (recipe on p. 112)

Tips:

- ❖ To facilitate quick movement through a buffet line, arrange buffet tables so that people can be served from both sides.
- ❖ Divide dishes into two bowls whenever possible and put one on each side of the buffet table. For larger containers, such as large aluminum trays of chicken salad, turn lengthwise and be sure to include serving spoons accessible to people on each side of the buffet line.

Church Lunch for 200

Mabel organized hundreds of lunches like this. Probably most of the folks in our congregation, where Mabel had been a member for about 60 years, can still remember the typical menu she would serve. Many came to expect it such that they would be disappointed if she chose to make any substitutions.

Strawberry Spinach Salad
Hot Chicken Salad
Tortellini Salad
Rolls with Butter
Sticky Buns
Costco Cookies or Cake
Lemonade and Water

Notes/Instructions

Strawberry Spinach Salad – 4 large bowls (recipe on p. 44)
Hot Chicken Salad – 4 large trays (recipe on p. 78)
Tortellini Salad – 2 large bowls (recipe on p. 81)
Rolls with Butter – 250-300 rolls
Sticky Buns – 6 trays (recipe on p. 112)
Cake or Cookies – 2 full sheet cakes, or enough cartons of cookies for 1 per person
Lemonade and Water

Wedding Fare for 250

One of the most memorable moments of Mabel's 100th birthday celebration was when Frank, as the emcee, asked the nearly 700 people in the church sanctuary which of them had a wedding reception catered by Mabel. Many hands went up. Frank added to the question: how many of your parents had a wedding reception catered by Mabel? And then, how many of your grandparents had a wedding reception catered by Mabel? Still more hands went up. Lastly, how many of you have attended a wedding reception catered by Mabel? Not one hand in that sanctuary remained down.

Most of those weddings were lovely, unpretentious affairs, where venue, food, and style took a back seat to the celebration of vows. Maybe some folks can remember what was served, but certainly all can recall the joy of the day. For Mabel, weddings were always an opportunity to call many hands together to contribute to the celebration. As she saw it, the more people were involved from the beginning, the harder it would ever be to dissolve that union. More than merely catering events, Mabel was using food to bind hearts.

<u>Appetizers</u>
Fruit Trays
Cheese and Cracker trays
Fresh Crab Dip
Meatballs
Spinach Artichoke Dip

<u>Dinner</u>
Hot or Cold Chicken Salad
Strawberry Spinach Salad

Tortellini Salad
Spiral Sliced Ham
Asparagus with Lemon Butter
Dinner Rolls with Butter
Sticky Buns

<u>Drinks</u>
Sparkling Water
Iced Tea
Coffee

<u>Dessert</u>
Wedding Cake

Notes/Instructions

If you are not a professional caterer (or even if you are Mabel with decades of catering experience but no professional kitchen), you will need to enlist plenty of help to pull off cooking for such a large crowd, mostly because of space and food storage constraints. Planning your exact menu will require some math, and if you're like me, will definitely require a double-check by your math savvy friends. There is plenty of help available to you out there on the Internet as well. Google and YouTube practically make us all pros! (One site you might find helpful is thekitch.com.) Although the menus I have provided here are reliable and Mabel-tested, you will nonetheless want to make sure you take into consideration all the factors of your particular event, such as the following:

- Age: Guys in their 20s for example, can inhale massive amounts of food in minutes, so if that demographic will make up a significant portion of your guest list, it would be best to prepare more than recommended.
- Time of day: Off-hours events generally require a little less food, but you never want your guests to feel hungry. The menu below is for a full dinner, but you could do an appetizer event during the dinner hour as long as you serve heavier hors d'oeuvres in greater amounts.
- Drinks: If you are serving alcohol, be sure that your menu includes some high protein and high carbohydrate choices.
- Consider what you might be able to purchase already prepared. Remember that you are considering not only actual cost, but labor and storage capacity. Purchased desserts are often quite lovely, for example.

- If you find that you are running short of one item, place that item as one of the last items on the buffet line as folks are mostly likely to fill up their plates with what they see first.

Appetizers

Fruit Trays - 5 trays (instructions on p. 123)
Cheese and Cracker Trays (instructions on p. 124)
Fresh Crab Dip – 5 recipes (recipe on p. 14)
Meatballs – 3 trays divided into five serving dishes (recipe on p. 15)

- Check big box stores for excellent versions of prepared meatballs. These can be thrown into crockpots and served warmed with minimal effort.

Spinach Artichoke Dip – 5 recipes (recipe on p. 17)

- Prepare the dip a day or two ahead and store in the refrigerator. Fill the hollowed-out baguettes on the day of the event. Using the bread as the serving vessel provides nice visual interest on your table.

Dinner

Hot or Cold Chicken Salad – 6 large bowls (recipe on p. 78-79)

- Events that are earlier in the day lend themselves more readily to a cold chicken salad. You will also want to take into account how much oven/warmer space you have to be sure that a hot chicken salad will be served warm, or how much fridge space you have to keep cold chicken salad cold.

Strawberry Spinach Salad – 4 large bowls (recipe on p. 44)

- The dressing for the salad can be mixed up days ahead and stored in jars or sealed plastic bags for up to a week. Strawberries can be sliced a day or two ahead and tossed with the salad on the day of the event.

Tortellini Salad – 5 large bowls (recipe on p. 81)
Spiral Sliced Hams – 5 8-10 lbs. each

- Look for sales throughout the year (especially after Easter) to buy and freeze.
- Hams can also be heated in crock pots if oven space is at a minimum.
- Brush with glaze (usually provided with the ham) to keep it moist, or make your own simple glaze: 2/3 c. brown sugar, ¼ c. orange or pineapple juice, and 2 tsbp. Dijon mustard.

Asparagus with Lemon Butter – 24 lbs. (recipe on p. 46)

- Double the recipe on p. 46. Make 6 recipes. Separate asparagus into 6 trays of about 4 pounds of asparagus each.

Dinner Rolls with butter

- Be sure to have at least 2 rolls per person.
- Make decorative butter rosettes by spreading room temperature butter into heart shaped silicone candy molds. Pop them out when solid and store in airtight containers. (I got this idea from thekitchn.com.)

Sticky Buns – 6 trays

Dessert
Wedding Cake

- A 10-inch round store bought cake (Costco has some of the most delicious options!) will serve at least 16 people. For an attractive display, put out a few cakes on pedestals of various heights on a round table, topped with posies of fresh flowers and surrounded by strands or greenery.
- For budget considerations, cut and serve these cakes first, and then supplement with (equally delicious) sheet cake that was sliced and plated out of sight of the guests.

Tips:

❖ Arrange appetizers on 5 separate round tables to prevent crowding and be sure everybody can access the food.

❖ In a buffet line, always place the meat as the final item at the end of the line. Folks will fill up on the other delicious dishes, and you'll be able to keep the cost more reasonable by encouraging them to first fill their plates with colorful and nutritious veggies, salads, and of course a nice buttery piece of bread. "It has to be practical as well as delicious!" she always said. "And there are a lot of people to get through that buffet line!"

❖ Do as much as you can ahead of time.
  • Dressings can always be made a couple days in advanced and stored in the fridge.
  • Chicken for chicken salad can be cooked ahead of time and even frozen in zip lock bags.

❖ Plan for prep to take 50% longer than you think it will. In the unlikely event you have some free time, you can relax!

❖ Keep lists, but be flexible. Expect that not everything will go according to plan, and just roll with it.

Weekend Youth Group Retreat for 75

If Mabel had a magnum opus, it may have been her work at the Camp Hemlock Labor Day Retreats. Mabel could be found in the West Virginia woods of this camp every year for at least 50 years. The menus below are the ones that we followed for the fifteen or so years we were Mabel's kitchen help at Hemlock. She was quite proud that "kids come to Labor Day because we don't serve ordinary camp food here!" Of course, there are groups of hungry teenagers in places other than the woods of West Virginia, so these menus can be used for any large gatherings, and will please palates of all ages.

Keep in mind that we work in a camp kitchen with three large ovens, two large griddles, a walk-in fridge and an industrial size mixer. The recipes/instructions listed here feed a crowd of about 75 people, usually including a fair number of active teenagers who have typically been running around outside all weekend. In other situations, and for other age groups, the amounts here will likely leave you with a lot of leftovers (which is not necessarily a bad thing).

Late Night Arrival Snack
Pizza

Day One

Breakfast
Bacon
Pancakes with Hot Syrup and Butter

Assorted cereal and milk
Greek Yogurt and Granola
Orange Juice

Lunch
Spaghetti and meatballs
French bread
Green salad
Iced Tea/Lemonade

Dessert
Sherbet

Dinner
Spiral Sliced Ham
Green beans
Roasted Red Potatoes
Applesauce
Iced Tea/Lemonade

Dessert
Hot Fudge Sundaes

Late Night Snack
Rosenfelder Dip

Day Two

Brunch
Egg Casserole
Pork Sausage
Sticky Buns
Hash Browns
Waffles
Chicken Salad

<u>Dinner</u>
Barbecued Babyback Ribs
French Fries
Ambrosia Salad
Green Salad

<u>Dessert</u>
Baked Alaska

<u>Late Night Snack</u>
'Smores around the campfire

Notes/Instructions

Arrival Day Snack

Pizza – 6 – 16 in. premade pizzas

- Prepare according to package directions. Slice into sections about 1/3 the size of a dinner slice portion. We have found that slicing into small squares rather than triangle slices has worked well.

Day One

Breakfast

Bacon – 16 pounds

- Cover baking sheets with parchment paper. Bake bacon at 375° for about 15-20 minutes, until crispy.
- Serve bacon on platters that include 2 slices per person. After that, campers can come seeking platter refills if desired.

Pancakes – 1 10 lb. bag of mix such as Krusteaz

- Prepare according to directions (using an electric mixer if available makes the fluffiest pancakes)
- Warm 2 64 oz. containers of syrup on medium heat on the stove, pour into small syrup dishes to serve
- Serve with ½ stick softened butter per each table of 6-8 people

146

Orange Juice

- 6 – 8 60 oz. containers (buying frozen and adding water is more budget friendly)

Assorted cereal and milk

- 4-6 large assorted boxes (Cheerios, Wheaties, Kashi Puffs)
- 1 gallon of whole milk
- 2 32 oz. vanilla Greek yogurt and 4 16 oz. packages of granola

Lunch

Spaghetti and meatballs – 2 6 lb. bags of frozen meatballs; 8 1 lb. boxes of spaghetti prepared according to directions on package

- In each of 2 large aluminum trays, combine the following:

  1 6 lb. bag of meatballs
  1 6 lb.15 oz. tomato sauce
  ½ can (same size) crushed tomatoes
  ½ can (same size) tomato paste

  Stir everything to combine and heat in the oven on med/low about 2 hours or until heated through, stirring occasionally. Season as desired.

- Serve with parmesan cheese

French bread – 8 loaves

- Slice loaf lengthwise down the middle and spread each side generously with softened butter. Season liberally with garlic salt. Put the loaf back together and slice into one-inch slices. Wrap in aluminum foil and toast in 350° oven for about 20 minutes. Cut into slices to serve.

Green salad

- Toss together the following and serve with your choice of salad dressing:
  2 16 oz. cartons mixed salad greens
  3 heads romaine or other artisan lettuce, chopped
  2 lb. box roma tomatoes, diced
  2 large seedless cucumbers, diced
  1 small bag sweet colored peppers, diced
  Sherbet – 4 gallons, various flavors

Dinner

(prepare according to directions on package)
Steamed Green Beans – 4 2 lb. bags (recipe on p. 48 adjusted below for numbers)

- Distribute beans among 3 aluminum trays filled with a couple of inches of water. Cover with foil and steam for about 20 minutes, until crisp tender, being careful that water does not boil off and beans do not scorch. When done, drain beans. Add about ½ a stick of butter and toss gently. Omit any nuts when serving children.

Roasted Red Potatoes – (recipe on p. 47)

- Prepare 2 5 lb. recipes.

Applesauce – 3 48 oz. containers

- Serve chilled and sprinkled with cinnamon.

Hot Fudge Sundaes - (recipe on p. 114) adapted below for a large crowd

- In a large pot on the stove, combine the following and heat slowly over low heat:
  12 14 oz. cans sweetened condensed mile
  2 bars unsweetened chocolate

2 bars semi-sweet chocolate

- Prepare 8 ½ gallon cartons of ice cream (or 4 gallon tubs) into individual servings. Serve warm sauce over ice cream. Cardboard cartons of ice cream can be opened and sliced into portions with a large knife more efficiently and evenly than scooping out of tub gallon containers.

<u>Late Night Snack</u>
Rosenfelder Dip (recipe on p. 15)

- Serve with two large (40 oz.) bags of tortilla chips.

Day Two

<u>Brunch</u>
Brunch Casserole – 2 recipes (recipe on p. 80)
Sausage Patties - 4 3.5 lb. bags

- Heat on a griddle, approximately 5 minutes per side

Sticky Buns - at least 4 large aluminum trays
Hash Brown Potatoes – 4 6 lb. bags

- Fry one bag at a time on the griddle.

Waffles – 2 60 count boxes

- Heat in oven on large foil-lined aluminum trays. Serve with warmed maple syrup.

Hot Chicken Salad – 2 trays (recipe on p. 78)
Fruit Salad

- Any combination of cut up fruit can be used for a fruit salad, of course. The following combination makes a salad large enough

to serve 75 people when accompanied by the other brunch menu items above:
1 small seedless watermelon
2 pineapples
2 lbs. strawberries
1 lb. blueberries
2 cantaloupes
2 lbs. grapes

❖ Set the diced watermelon aside in a colander to drain and add to the salad immediately before serving. This will prevent the watermelon from making the rest of the salad soggy.
❖ For a pretty presentation, set aside about 10 whole strawberries, several kiwi slices, and about ½ c. of blueberries. Arrange the strawberries and kiwi slices alternately around the perimeter of the bowl and sprinkle the blueberries in the center.

Mid-day Snack

With only two meals served on this day, a snack is usually appreciated. We typically serve:

• One large, whole watermelon, sliced.
• A variety of granola bars, one per person

Dinner

Barbecued Babyback Ribs - 25 racks of ribs (usually sold 2 per package)
3 – 5 lb. containers of Sweet Baby Ray's Barbecue Sauce

• Using a large, sharp knife or kitchen scissors, cut ribs into servings of 2 ribs each. Place ribs in Large stock pots full of water. Boil gently for about 3 hrs., or until meat becomes tender. Arrange ribs in single layers on large foil covered aluminum trays. Brush liberally with barbecue sauce. Heat in 350° oven for approximately ½ hour.

French Fries – 4 8 lb. bags

- In batches small enough to spread French fries in a single layer, fry on the heated, oiled griddle until slightly browned and crisp, about 15 minutes. Season with salt to taste.

Ambrosia Salad

- Following is a large serving adaptation of the recipe on p. 45:

In a large mixing bowl, prepare 8 packages of orange jello according to package instructions.

Add 1 6 lb. can of tropical fruit (without the juice) and 4 11 oz. cans of apricot nectar. Put in the fridge to set. Because this is a large amount, it will usually take about 2 hours.

When set, stir in 2 12 oz. containers of cool whip.
Green Salad – see above Day One lunch
Corn on the Cob – one ear per person

- Fill a large pot of water and add a couple of tbsp. of salt and 1/8 c. sugar. Bring the water to a rolling boil, add corn and boil for 7 minutes.

Baked Alaska – (recipe on p. 114)

- Each pie serves 8 people generously. For our typical Labor Day sized crowd, we make 10 pies. Leftovers (when that happens) can easily be wrapped in plastic wrap and frozen for the next day.

<u>Late Night Snack</u>

Smores

- 4 bags of marshmallows, 8 boxes of graham crackers, and 2 36-count boxes of Hershey's chocolate bars.

Break each graham cracker in half, top with roasted marshmallow, ½ chocolate bar and top with the other half of the graham cracker.

- We have tried two methods of preparation according to the wishes of the camp director:

  1) Kitchen staff preferred method: Pack a bag with all the supplies and send them out to the campfire. Kids get the experience of roasting their own marshmallows under the stars. Kitchen staff relaxes.

  2) Camp director preferred method: Line a large aluminum tray with foil. Line up graham cracker halves and top with ½ of a chocolate bar and a marshmallow. Bake in 325 oven for about 15 minutes, until marshmallows are soft. Take out of oven and top with other graham cracker half. Have responsible campers carry cooled trays down to the campfire.

Tips:

- ❖ With the occurrence of various food allergies on the rise, it is best to avoid serving any dishes with nuts.
- ❖ The menus above represent a fair amount of variety. Those with varying dietary tastes or needs should be able to find something appropriate for them. It is advisable, still, to let campers know that if they are unable to eat the meals that are planned, there is plenty of fridge space available for them to bring their own meals.
- ❖ Kids (and adults!) need to stay hydrated. Large thermoses of powdered iced tea and lemonade are mixed up for each meal, and thermoses of ice water should always be available for folks to fill their own water bottles.

Day Three Adios Brunch

This meal is a smorgasbord of leftovers. In addition to heating up the leftovers, we typically have some eggs remaining to make scrambled eggs.

If there is any ham still left from Saturday night dinner, we dice it to serve in the scrambled eggs. Any leftover meatballs are heated to be served as meatball subs on sub rolls. Many campers have told us that this ends up being their favorite meal of the weekend.

Photo Credit: Karen Myers Frank

Epilogue

Leopard Print in Heaven

Tomorrow morning at church, the seat to my left will be achingly empty. This is Mabel's seat. We knew that, at 103, Mabel's days among us were growing short. Still, most of us were oddly shocked to hear that she had passed away. After all, she had asked the Lord for 105 and seemed pretty confident that He planned to comply. But as it turned out, He wanted her home.

Despite these brief impulses to grieve the empty spaces left by Mabel's home-going, though, the exchanges among her friends and family have been peppered by sparks of joyful reminiscences of her sticky buns, her sassy attitude, and her servant's heart. Mabel served others as naturally as most of us get up and walk around. In addition to the work she did feeding thousands of people across the metro D.C. area well past her 100th birthday, Mabel had an impeccable radar that sought out opportunities to give gifts to other people: frilly dresses for the pastor's children, ballerina figurines for the aspiring dancer, sandwiches for the tired mom with a new baby.

Even last Sunday, Easter Sunday, the day most of us will remember as the time we last saw Mabel, she had gifts for Frank and me, just because. She pulled this particular Lennox platter out of her bag, and in between snippets of conversation with dozens of people (did we know this would be our last chance?), told me that this one would go nicely with the other she had gifted me on another Sunday. She wanted me to have it because she knew that we love to have a houseful of people for Christmas, and no matter what I serve, "it should always look pretty!"

For Frank, she would frequently bring sports trinkets. This time, it was a New York Yankees tie. More than once, Mabel felt the need to detail for me the reasons she found Frank to be one of the wisest, most capable men she knew. She knew that in all the busy-ness and tedium that often marks our days on this earth, I needed reminders of the tremendous blessing it is to walk through life with someone like Frank. Her admiration of him is an unexpected gift, one that I didn't realize she was leaving me until now, after she is gone.

When I think of the moment that Mabel left us, when the thin veil between life and eternity was rent for her, I imagine her entrance to the other side to be like that of Sarah Smith in C.S. Lewis' *The Great Divorce.* Sarah Smith, one of the "great ones" in Heaven, had been a rather ordinary person in her life on Earth, yet now was attended by "a thousand liveried angels." She had no outstanding accomplishments to boast about, nor any remarkable talents to set her apart. Yet the things she did arose from a heart of genuine love for others. Because of that love, Sarah Smith has thousands of sons and daughters there, in that "country." Mabel too, I imagine, was greeted by multitudes of sons and daughters, those in whose lives she invested so lovingly…:" (Lewis 119). Sarah Smith was arrayed in splendor, her "innermost spirit [shining] through [her] clothes" (Lewis 118). Though no less resplendent, Mabel's heavenly garb, I suspect, is leopard print.

Like Sarah Smith, Mabel was an ordinary person, doing ordinary things. She came to D.C. from her Iowa farm to fulfill her patriotic duty during WWII. Then, she fed people. Like most of us, she did not possess unusual power or talent. But what she did, she did out of extraordinary love and obedience to God. Although she admittedly did not mind being the center of attention from time to time, all that Mabel did flowed from immense gratitude for what God had done for her. And thus she was perhaps one of the most joyful people we knew.

What a privilege it has been for so, so many of us to be witnesses to this long life that testifies to the power of God to do extraordinary things with ordinary people. Thanks be to God, the ache of the empty seat will last but a fleeting moment. Any thought of mourning will be eclipsed by the knowledge that our Mabel's joy is now complete.

"The thing of it is," Mabel would say, "God is just so good all the time."

April, 2017

Acknowledgements

Thanks to Mabel for sharing her time and her talents with so many for so long, and for giving many of us the courage to practice hospitality, and for sharing with us her zeal for doing God's work.

I so appreciate input from my English teacher colleagues and friends on this project. Thank you to Callie Feyen for your invaluable feedback, and for pointing me to the joy and nuance of story. Michelle Iskra used precious summer vacation time to offer helpful critique. Even more importantly, you have been a steadfast inspiration and motivation over the years.

Thanks to my talented brother-in-law, Mike Vail, for contributing the sketches made for photographs of Mabel's belongings.

Our Camp Hemlock teammate (and former student turned English teacher friend), Mary Troxel, reviewed recipes and menus. Mary is our most loyal Camp Hemlock partner, a fellow lover of language, literature, and story, and the quickest sticky bun maker to ever roll some dough.

To Mabel's nephew and his family: Dick and Doreen, Shanna, Megan and Sean, thank you for welcoming me as part of your family as you laid Mabel to rest at home in Iowa. As Sean told me, if I really wanted to know Mabel, I needed to experience her roots. I did, indeed, grow to know her better as you brought me with you to the land and the farm that she so loved. Her legacy lives on in all of you.

Mom and Dad became "Hemlockers" and bosom buddies of Mabel later in life and caught the vision of sharing her story. Besides that, they believe I can do almost anything. Thanks, Mom and Dad, for seeing what I cannot see. If I have any confidence in what I can do, it has grown from the seeds you planted decades ago and continued to cultivate along the way.

The person who helped me most to make this book into something I dared publish is my daughter, Alexandra Howe. Thank you dear daughter, for spending many hours reviewing and re-working narratives, all while you still held down your own full-time job and cared for the small human who lives with you whom we all love so dearly. Your keen ear for story, your heart to find beauty in language, and your professional editor's eye brought clarity and life to the manuscript. You are a gift; I admire you and I love you!

And, of course, thanks to my #1 fan and husband, Frank, for listening to me for several years agonizing over finishing this project. You are my rock and my inspiration. It is from you that I have learned how to walk into the fear of failing and just start working. No doubt Mabel will wonder what took so long. But what a grand reunion we will all have someday!

CPSIA information can be obtained
at www.ICGtesting.com
Printed in the USA
LVHW010447131222
735100LV00003B/76